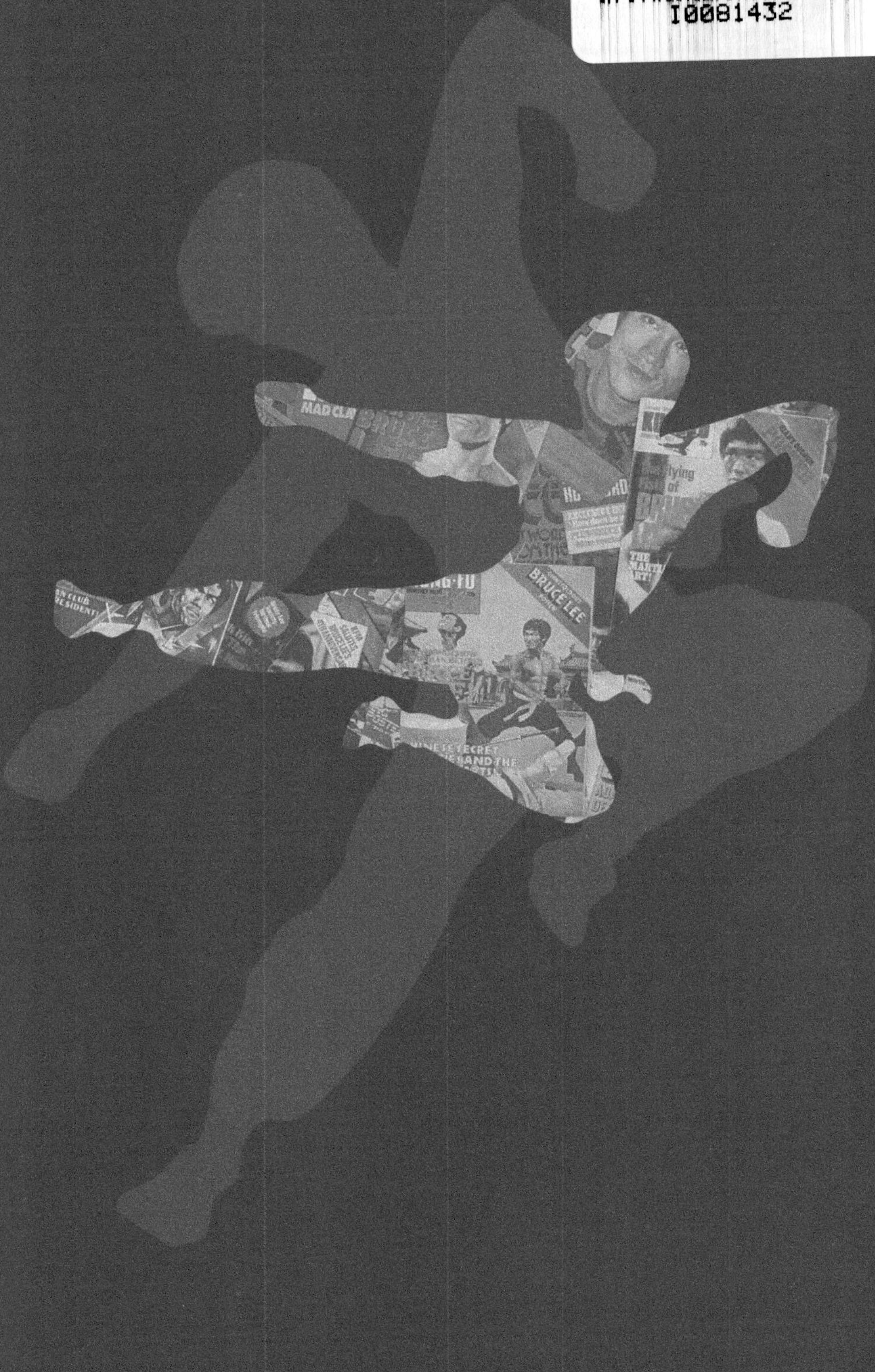
BRUCE LEE

FOLD-OUT BRUCE LEE POSTER INSIDE
PAGES OF FANTASTIC ACTION PIX
KUNG-FU
MONTHLY No.34
BRUCE LEE
AND THE SAVAGING OF THE MAD CLAW
MONTHLY No.12
EXCLUSIVE
BRUCE LEE
Really Like?
25p
FOLD OUT POSTER!
KFM SALUTES BRUCE LEE'S 4TH ANNIVERSARY!
WHERE IS THE MAGIC IN

KUNG-FU
MONTHLY

THE ARCHIVE SERIES

THE SECRET ART
OF BRUCE LEE

BY THE EDITORS OF
KUNG-FU MONTHLY

COMPILED AND EDITED BY
CARL FOX

PIT WHEEL PRESS
BARNSLEY

Published by
PIT WHEEL PRESS LIMITED
www.pitwheelpress.com

THE SECRET ART OF BRUCE LEE

A Pit Wheel Press edition, published by special
arrangement with Dennis Publishing, London.

First Printing 1976
Revised Edition 2022

Printed in the United Kingdom
ISBN 978-1-915414-16-8

DEDICATED TO

TAKY KIMURA AND DAN INOSANTO

*TWO LEAVES ON THE SAME BRANCH
OF BRUCE LEE'S SECRET ART.*

ACKNOWLEDGEMENTS

*I would like to thank the following people for their help
and participation in the making of this book:*

James Bishop	**John Overall**
Andrew Kimura	**Carlotta Serantoni**
John Little	**Andrew Staton**

Special Thanks
Tim Tackett

CREDITS

Original 1976 Edition

**Don Atyeo, Paul Simmons, Jonathon Green, Peter Bennett
Cathay Films (UK), Golden Harvest Films (Hong Kong)
Warner Bros Films (UK), Concord Films (Hong Kong)
Chang Vung Djih, Paul Chang & Rex Features Ltd.**
Black & White Photographs by **Chester Maydole.**
Design by **Perry Neville.** *Filmsetting by* **Letterbox Ltd.**

The Kung-Fu Monthly Archive Series

Research, Editing, Layout & Design
Carl Fox

Editorial Assistance
George Fox

Photograph Acknowlegements
Kung-Fu Monthly & Carl Fox

KUNG-FU

MONTHLY

THE ARCHIVE SERIES

THE SECRET ART
OF BRUCE LEE

CHAPTERS

ABOUT THE KFM ARCHIVE SERIES   11

FOREWORD BY TIM TACKETT   15

THE STORY OF THE MAYDOLE PHOTOS   21

THE MAYDOLE PHOTOGRAPHS
AN INTRODUCTION   27

01   BRUCE LEE THE MARTIAL ARTIST   35

STREET FIGHTER   37

STUDENT FIGHTER   41

A PHILOSOPHY   45

A NEW LAND   48

A NEW STYLE   56

02   JEET KUNE DO   65

UNDERSTANDING JEET KUNE DO   67

TRAINING   69

TRAINING WITH PARTNERS   88

STANCE   90

ESSENTIAL ELEMENTS   91

ATTACK   107

FOLD-OUT BRUCE LEE POSTER INSIDE
KUNG-FU MONTHLY
BRUCE LEE
AND THE SAVAGING OF THE MAD CLAW
EXCLUSIVE
FOLD OUT POSTER!
KFM SALUTES BRUCE LEE'S 4TH ANNIVERSARY!
UNBEATABLE JEET KUNE DO
WHERE IS THE MAGIC IN

KUNG-FU
MONTHLY

THE ARCHIVE SERIES
ABOUT THE SERIES

FOLD-OUT
BRUCE LEE
POSTER INSIDE
PAGES OF FANTASTIC ACTION PIX
AND THE
SAVAGING
OF THE
MAD CLAW
KUNG-FU
MONTHLY No.34
BRUCE
LEE
EXCLUSIVE
BRUCE
LEE
KUNG-FU
No.9
25p
FOLD
OUT POSTER!
UNBEATABLE
Ultimate
Bruce Lee Society 1st Year Triumph!
KFM
SALUTES
BRUCE LEE'S
4TH ANNIVERSARY!
WHERE IS THE MAGIC IN

Kung-Fu Monthly is a name synonymous with Bruce Lee, not only in the United Kingdom but throughout the world. It is a legend in its own right and a brand immediately recognisable by not only the font but also the famous "flying man" logo.

The popularity of the magazine at the peak of the Kung Fu Craze in the 1970s was unrivalled and its success was almost entirely down to pure luck.

Legend has it that *Kung-Fu Monthly* began life as a gamble by underground comic book publisher Felix Dennis after questioning a queue of kids outside a Soho cinema, waiting to see *Enter the Dragon* in early 1974. On paper, the idea seemed to serve the then-current trend of Bruce Lee and was deemed to have a shelf life of three to six months but a year after its launch, *Kung-Fu Monthly* had become the biggest-selling Bruce Lee magazine in the world.

After the demise of the Official Bruce Lee Fan Club in 1976, *Kung-Fu Monthly* launched their own. The KFM Bruce Lee Society ran for thirty quarterly newsletters from 1976 to 1983 and at the time of closing, had seen over five thousand eager Bruce Lee fans become members throughout its tenure, with the formidable Pam Hadden at the forefront throughout its seven active years.

Kung-Fu Monthly and The Bruce Lee Society were jointly responsible for the UK's first Bruce Lee Convention held on May 19th 1979 and the first Bruce Lee Film Festival held on December 1st 1979.

Kung-Fu Monthly and later *Personal Computer World*, had turned H. Bunch Associates from an underground publisher on the verge of bankruptcy to a publishing powerhouse, eventually becoming Dennis Publishing, named after its founder, Felix Dennis.

That leads us to today.

In February 2021, I approached Dennis Publishing with an idea for a project that I'd thought of doing for many years - scan, convert, edit and compile all seventy-nine issues of the iconic *Kung-Fu Monthly* magazine into book form, in order to present it to a new audience, as well as preserve its place in history.

It was the longest-running dedicated Bruce Lee magazine of its kind anywhere in the world (by frequency and circulation) and I wanted to pay homage to that. Such was its success and popularity that it was licensed throughout the world; in fourteen countries and in eleven languages. That doesn't even take into account the non-official bootlegs which appeared in China and Turkey. Nothing has matched it before or since. It truly has stood the test of time and having done so, has reached legendary status.

Kung-Fu Monthly is a snapshot of a time long gone; a time which the original fans remember with fondness and a time which new fans will hopefully discover.

The *Kung-Fu Monthly Archive Series* is dedicated to Felix Dennis and everyone associated with the magazine; not just the staff but also the fans, who would buy copies of the magazines in their millions over its lifetime and help cement the publication's place in British Pop Culture history.

Special thanks must also go to Carlotta Serantoni at Dennis Publishing for her assistance in allowing this project to go ahead.

Carl Fox
February 2022

KUNG MONTHLY NO.12

AND THE SAVAGING OF THE MAD CLAW

KARATE

FOLD-OUT BRUCE LEE POSTER INSIDE

PAGES OF FANTASTIC ACTION PIX

EXCLUSI

What W BRUCE LEE Really Like?

The KFM I

KUNG-FU MONTHLY NO.

BRUCE LEE

KUNG-FU NO.9 25p

FOLD OUT POSTER!

UNBEATA FEET Ultimate A

KC MONTHLY

Bruce Lee Secretary Bit Years Triumph

KFM SALUTES BRUCE LEE'S 4TH ANNIVERSARY!

FANTASTIC KICK POSTER OFFER OUT!

CHI SOC MA

WHERE IS THE MAGIC IN
The Bruce Lee series

KUNG-FU
MONTHLY

THE ARCHIVE SERIES
THE SECRET ART
OF BRUCE LEE

FOREWORD

I started taking Jeet Kune Do at Dan Inosanto's backyard gym in 1971 shortly after Bruce Lee had moved to Hong Kong to make his first martial art film. I was aware of Bruce Lee around 1967. I knew that he was in *The Green Hornet*. I saw the TV episode of Longstreet where Bruce Lee talks about the art he teaches called Jeet Kune Do. I had also read some Black Belt Magazine articles by him about Jeet Kune Do and had seen him do a demonstration at a karate seminar. All of this made me want to study this art. I had studied Chinese martial arts in Taiwan had a school in Redlands, California to help pay for college. While I was interested in learning Jeet Kune Do, I had no time to drive seventy miles to study at Bruce Lee's Los Angeles Chinatown school.

When I finished college and started teaching high school, I finally had the time to train in Jeet Kune Do, but by that time Bruce Lee had closed his school and moved to Hong Kong. I found out that his main assistant, Dan Inosanto had a small group training Jeet Kune Do in a small backyard gym.

At that time, people who watched *The Green Hornet* could only remember the character of Kato, and few could remember the actor's name.

It wasn't until Bruce passed away that he became a worldwide celebrity. Then everybody wanted to know about the famous actor's life. The search was on for any writing that

The Jeet Kune Do Backyard Group circa 1970s: *(Left to Right)* Tim Tackett, Dan Inosanto, Richard Bustillo, Dan Lee, Jerry Poteet, Bob Bremer and Pete Jacobs. *Photograph Courtesy of Tim Tackett.*

Bruce Lee had done and any photos that could be found. Many magazine articles were written. If a publisher wanted to sell his magazine, he put Bruce Lee on the cover.

Some of his notes were published under the title of The Tao of Jeet Kune Do. His book Chinese Gung Fu published in 1963 was reprinted. A collection of photos taken for a possible book was found in a box and published in four volumes called Bruce Lee's Fighting Method. In the late 1990's, The Bruce Lee Educational Foundation came into existence, and John Little was able to go through all of Bruce Lee's notes which were published in a multi-volume series. One was a book called the Tao of Gung Fu.

It is now 2021 and you would think that there is nothing more to be discovered, but you would be wrong. The archive of the UK's Kung-Fu Monthly Magazine has just been complied by Carl Fox. In it were discovered photos of Bruce Lee and Dan Inosanto taken in 1967 for a possible book. These photos were taken a year or two before the ones in the Fighting Method books. The photos and text from The Secret Art of Bruce Lee has been re-edited by Carl Fox as part of the Kung-Fu Monthly Archive Series. The Secret Art of Bruce Lee is a must for anyone interested in Bruce Lee or the art of Jeet Kune Do.

Tim Tackett
June 2021

Photograph Courtesy of Tim Tackett.

KUNG-FU
MONTHLY

THE ARCHIVE SERIES
THE SECRET ART
OF BRUCE LEE

FOLD-OUT BRUCE LEE POSTER INSIDE

PAGES OF FANTASTIC ACTION PIX

KARA CHU

WORLD'S BEST SELL
KUNG
MONTHLY No.12

AND THE SAVAGING OF THE MAD CLA

EXCLUSI
What W
BRUC
LEE
Really Like?
The KFM I

KUNG-FU
MONTHLY No.14
15p
BRUCE LEE

KUNG-FU
No.9
25p

FOLD OUT POSTER!

UNBEATA
GET A
Ultimate

WORLD'S
KU
MONTH

E WITH
CE
E

Bruce Lee
Screen
1st Year
Triumph

KFM
SALUTES
BRUCE LEE'S
4TH ANNIVERSARY!

K Kin
THE
than

FANTAS
KICK
POSTER OFFER
OUT!

POSTE
PA

CHI
SOC
MA

WHERE IS THE MAGIC IN
The Bruce Lee Secret

KUNG-FU
MONTHLY

THE ARCHIVE SERIES
THE SECRET ART
OF BRUCE LEE

INTRODUCTION

THE SECRET ART OF
BRUCE LEE

Over 100 Previously Unpublished Photographs of Bruce Lee in Action!

By the Editors of Kung-Fu Monthly, Photographs by Chester Maydole.

In 1965, a twenty five year old Bruce Lee has been in the USA for six years, having been sent there from Hong Kong by his father in 1959 after repeatedly getting into fights. After setting up his Jun Fan Gung Fu school, Lee has started attracting famous students such as celebrity hairstylist Jay Sebring.

One of Sebring's clients was William Dozier, the producer of the popular TV show *Batman*, based on the comic book of the same name. Sebring commented to Dozier that he should check out Lee at a local martial arts tournament being held by Ed Parker in Long Beach, California. On 12th June 1965, Bruce Lee walked into the studios of Twentieth Century Fox to participate in a screen test for a new series being developed by Dozier entitled *Number One Son*, about the son of Charlie Chan, the popular fictional Chinese-American detective from several novels and movies from the 1940s and 50s.

Just over two months before the screen test, Lee had become a father to Brandon, the first child between his wife Linda and himself. The director of the screen test tells Lee that he understands he just had a baby boy and asked if he has lost any sleep recently, to which Lee replies, "Three nights!" Unfortunately for Lee at the time, *Number One Son* was never made. When asked six years later by Canadian broadcaster Pierre Berton if it has been made, Lee replied, "No. They were going to make it into a new Chinese James Bond type of a thing. Now that, you know, the old man Chan is dead. Charlie is dead, and his son is carrying on." After missing out on *Number One Son*, Lee returned to teaching martial arts.

A year after the Number One Son screen test, William Dozier was developing a new TV series based on the comic book *The Green Hornet*. Success with another comic book TV series *Batman*, Dozier attempted to cash in on that success by bringing *The Green Hornet* to the small screen. Having already been a hit on radio, *The Green Hornet* was the perfect candidate for the TV treatment and although Dozier didn't have an actor in mind for the lead role of Britt Reid, he knew exactly who he wanted for his Kung Fu fighting chauffeur Kato – Bruce Lee. The role of Kato was actually cast before that of Britt Reid/The Green Hornet as evidenced in several Green Hornet screen tests, where Lee's Kato is seen reading lines with several potential Green Hornets. Eventually, Van Wiiliams was cast in the lead role and confirmed the casting timeline. "I think Bruce was already gotten when I was brought on board," remembered Van Williams. "They still hadn't got The Green Hornet but they had got Kato. I don't think I met Bruce until the press party. Adam West introduced us both and we were there and it was the first time I'd met Bruce and we didn't really have much time to sit down and talk or anything else. He was really a very personal guy." Lee later joked on the reason behind his casting, "I was the only Chinese man in California who could pronounce, 'Britt Reid.'" Van Williams commented in a 1992 interview how Bruce would sometimes struggle with pronouniation, "His biggest problem was that he had a very thick Chinese accent that was very hard to understand and a lot of the lines he read a lot of the people just couldn't understand. So slowly but surely they took a lot of his lines away to the point where it was that he mostly did action stuff and whatever." Lee wasn't entirely happy with his performance in *The Green Hornet* as he told Pierre Berton in 1971, "I did a really terrible job in that, I have to say."

The first episode of *The Green Hornet* was aired on US TV on 9th September 1966. As a pre-planned advertisement, *The Green Hornet* and Kato would make a cameo appearance in *The Spell of Tut*, the ninth episode in the second season of *Batman* which aired on

28th September 1966.

The Green Hornet was a moderate success, though not as successful as William Dozier's other series, *Batman*. In order to increase ratings, it was decided to write some more episodes where the worlds of *Batman* and *The Green Hornet* would join together. *A Piece of the Action* and *Batman's Satisfaction* initially had the duos facing off against each other before joining forces to fight crime.

With Lee now a TV star, the studios had photographers take various publicity shots on and off set; one of those photographers being Chester Maydole.

Chester Maydole was born in 1923 moved to Los Angeles in 1947 after the Second World War in order to pursue a career in the arts. He became interested in photography while visiting a film set, he became interested in photography and began to photograph his neighbours, one of those being Clint Eastwood. In his later career, he began taking portfolio pictures for actors and models. Maydole built up a strong working relationship with actor Steve McQueen as well as photographing actresses Sally Field, Mia Farrow, Raquel Welch and Sharon Tate.

The American Jazz Pianist Les McCann wrote of Maydole, "I think of Chester as my early technique teacher for photography because when I was working in Hollywood, I would go up to his house (each night, after I got out of work) and we'd meet in his darkroom after hours. Over a period of a year or two, I would watch him. It was fantastic. I did my own developing, my own printing, and I learned it all from him. He was a great photographer as well. He took all those cowboy pictures of me."

As stated in *The Secret Art of Bruce Lee*, "At that time, Maydole was working as a 'photographer to the stars,' taking assignments from major film and television studios in Hollywood who needed publicity shots of their actors and actresses."

Maydole recalled, "I'd done some shots of *Batman*, which was very successful at that time, and I was asked by the company to take pictures of Bruce Lee and Van Williams. They were for the fan magazines as I recall."

Maydole photographed Lee in four sessions at four separate locations - Portuguese Bend in South Los Angeles, Lee's apartment in West Los Angeles, Malibu Beach, and Batman star Adam West's beach house in Palos Verdes.

Maydole found Lee extremely easy to work with and very enthusiastic about his new career and was eager to help in any way. "He'd done pictures in Hong Kong before, but I suppose he was making a lot more money now and it must have been quite a thing, a half-hour show which might run for a long time. It didn't, of course, but he wasn't to know that." During the shooting session, both Lee and Maydole enjoyed their professional relationship and they quickly became friends.

"He was a terrific guy," recalled Maydole. "I liked him very much. He was smart - not Hollywood smart, but he really knew his stuff. He was a very natural and down-to-earth sort of person. He didn't take much part in the usual Hollywood goings on; he was more interested in his martial arts. He was a very spiritual person and I know he meditated a lot. After all, Kung Fu is a very heavy thing, especially if you are Chinese and you have all that tradition behind you. It sort of becomes a religion. Yet it's a funny thing that, although Bruce went in for the whole thing, he taught just the opposite. He taught that people don't have to follow ritual. He taught you shouldn't be bound - you should be free."

Maydole remembered Lee as being obsessed with martial arts. He said he was always exercising, constantly performing impromptu movements and the only time he was still, was when he was engrossed in a book from his enormous library.

"I can't say enough about his Kung Fu and his teachings," said Maydole. "I had great respect for him. He had probably the most perfect body I have ever seen. He was small - perhaps 140 pounds - but his physique was most unusual, especially for a Chinese. He worked on it all the time. He was very particular about what he ate. He ate a lot of Chinese food, naturally enough, cooked specially for him by one or two of the Chinese restaurants in Chinatown. I remember how he would sit there eating this special food with all his students around him, holding court."

With his TV career going well, it wasn't long before Lee considered resuming his martial arts career and after looking around the city for a suitable place, he opened a Kung Fu school in Chinatown. Maydole recalled Lee's decision causing waves within the community. "Nobody had ever taught Kung Fu here before. Several top Karate black belts such as Danny Inosanto went over to Bruce and there was a lot of jealousy among the Karate people who said that Kung Fu didn't mean anything. Bruce challenged them on several occasions, but nothing ever came of it. I suppose they knew in their hearts how good he was."

Despite their friendship, Maydole wasn't overly convinced of the self-defence aspect of Lee's martial arts and was concerned about its potentially violent potential. What concerned him more was Lee's deadly expertise in the art. "Bruce had this big wooden dummy which he would use, and once he showed me 52 ways of kicking it. By kicking on a certain place you could blind a person, cripple him, kill him - whatever you chose. And Bruce, with his big toe, he could kick in any one of those 52 places. He was always wearing bare feet or ballet shoes so he could use his toe more freely. His big toe was a lethal weapon. He could kick you with it on the chin from any direction without warning."

In one photography session, Lee and his student Dan Inosanto met with Maydole at *Batman* star Adam West's beach house in Palos Verdes, as confirmed by Inosanto several years later. There is a possibility that some of the photographs – especially the ones taken near West's beach house – were taken by Maydole for a proposed martial arts book collaboration between Lee and West to take advantage of their success on *The Green Hornet* and *Batman* respectively.

Although he never fully trained with him, Maydole was immensely impressed with Lee's skills and soon realised that they would look good on film. The result of that are the photographs in *The Secret Art of Bruce Lee*. "They were taken," recalled Maydole, "just for the hell of it. I thought that with a little pushing, I could sell some of them to a Karate magazine, and so the first of four sessions was set up." On Malibu Beach, Lee and his pupil, Dan Inosanto, ran through a series of attacks and defences in front of Chester Maydole's lens.

Other photographs were taken in Lee's Los Angeles apartment and depict some of Lee's training methods and equipment, plus a section of his vast martial arts library and weapons collection. They represent a small glimpse of Lee the family man realising his dream on the cusp of stardom.

"Bruce was very proud of his wife and young son Brandon," remembered Maydole. "His other child was born after we lost contact with each other. Linda was very quiet. She never said a word which made her rather hard to get to know. Maybe she had decided to take a backseat to Bruce because he was the star. She was a martial artist herself though. And Brandon should be very good at Kung Fu when he grows up, too. Even at that age he was learning."

Unfortunately, Maydole never sold the photographs he took of Lee but his photography career continued upwards and he found himself very much in demand, photographing celebrities such as Farah Fawcett and Lee's old student Steve McQueen. Due to time constraints, they lost contact with each other, although Lee often contacted Maydole to discuss the book project in which he intended to use the photographer's photographs as illustrations. With Maydole tied up travelling the world with work, Lee stopped calling him. "It was just circumstances," recalled Maydole sadly. "Both of us were trying to make a living and, of course, I'm really sorry I didn't do the book."

Having not been used, the photographs that Maydole took were stored away. "I stuck them in my dead picture file and forgot about them," said Maydole. "Then recently my agent mentioned he was after pictures of Bruce Lee. I said I had lots of shots of Bruce doing Kung Fu. And that was that."

After being out of print for over forty years, and with permission from Dennis Publishing, *The Secret Art of Bruce Lee* has been re-released for not only Lee's fans, but also for historical preservation and education of future generations.

Carl Fox
June 2022

THE MAYDOLE
PHOTOGRAPHS
INTRODUCTION

Young Man.
Seize every minute.
Of your time.
The days fly by;
Ere long you too.
Will grow old.

POEM BY TZU YEH
TRANSLATED BY BRUCE LEE

The book you are holding represents a milestone in the history of the martial arts. It is the sole surviving photographic record of Bruce Lee's Jeet Kune Do as demonstrated by Lee himself. Forgotten for more than a decade, the photographs shown here - for the first time ever - have now come to be recognised as probably the finest illustration of his martial art that Bruce Lee has left us. To Lee's countless fans around the globe they will prove of enormous interest; as a visual aid for the student of the martial arts, they are invaluable.

Although at the time of his death Bruce Lee had reached the pinnacle of success in two spheres of achievement - films and the martial arts - he left little in the way of a tangible legacy. Unfortunately, most of Lee's fame and exposure came with the release of his films in the Western world after his death. All that is left of his extraordinary acting career are four films of varying quality, twenty minutes or so of a fifth, uncompleted film, and a handful of taped or written interviews.

From his martial art career even less survives. At the time of his death Lee was working on a book setting out his thoughts on the martial arts 'style' he had created - Jeet Kune Do. To be called the Too of Jeet Kune Do, this book was to have been a distillation of seven volumes of notes and writings that Lee had compiled in his last years. Since his death, Lee's widow, Linda, has overseen the cataloguing of these volumes and the Tao has now been published. As a written record of the processes of Jeet Kune Do it is excellent; nevertheless it is, unfortunately, far from the definitive work one would have expected if Lee had lived to finish his work.

Besides the Tao of Jeet Kune Do, Lee also left a few brief interviews - notably with Black Belt Magazine - in which he discussed Jeet Kune Do. These, together with the instructions he gave his pupils, are all that remain to guide the student along Lee's path to martial mastery. No films of Lee in action except, of course, the obviously stagey and exaggerated feature movies' were ever taken, and still photographs have hitherto been of little value, concentrating in the main on Lee's movie-star face and features rather than on his art.

It is therefore a stroke of unbelievable good fortune that the photographs hi this book have been rediscovered. That they could have remained in obscurity for so many years, considering the world-wide demand for any Lee material since his death in 1973, is nothing short of incredible.

The history of the photographs dates back to California, 1966. They were taken by a freelance Hollywood photographer named Chester Maydole during four shooting sessions at three separate locations - Portuguese Bend in South Los Angeles, Lee's apartment in West Los Angeles, and the famous Malibu Beach. At that time, Maydole was working as a 'photographer to the stars', taking assignments from major film and television studios in Hollywood who needed publicity shots of their actors and actresses. He first met Bruce Lee on the latter's arrival in Hollywood to make his television debut as Kato in the ill-fated Green Hornet series.

"I'd done some shots of Batman, which was very successful at that time," remembers Maydole, who now lives in New Mexico, "and I was asked by the company to take pictures of Bruce and Van Williams. They were for the fan magazines as I recall.

Maydole found Lee extremely easy to work with. Lee was bubbling over with excitement about his new career and was eager to help in any way. "He'd done pictures in Hong Kong before, but I suppose he was making a lot more money now and it must have been quite a thing, a half-hour show which might run for a long time. It didn't, of course, but he wasn't to know that. "During the course of the session the two men struck up a happy working relationship which quickly turned to friendship.

"He was a terrific guy," recalls Maydole. "I liked him very much. He was smart - not Hollywood smart, but he really knew his stuff. He was a very natural and down-to-earth sort of person. He didn't take much part in the usual Hollywood goings on; he was more interested in his martial arts. He was a very spiritual person and I know he meditated a lot. After all, Kung-Fu is a very heavy thing, especially if you are Chinese and you have all that tradition behind you. It sort of becomes a religion. Yet it's a funny thing that, although Bruce went in for the whole thing, he taught just the opposite. He taught that people don't have to follow ritual. He taught you shouldn't be bound - you should be free." Which, as we shall see later, was the very essence of Jeet Kune Do.

Maydole remembers Lee as being obsessed with the martial arts, living Kung-Fu twenty-four hours a day. He was always exercising, constantly performing impromptu movements. The only time he was still was when he was engrossed in a book from his enormous martial arts library.

'I can't say enough about his Kung-Fu and his teachings," says Maydole. "I had great respect for him. He had probably the most perfect body I have ever seen. He was small - perhaps 140 pounds - but his physique was most unusual, especially for a Chinese. He worked on it all the time. He was very particular about what he ate. He ate a lot of Chinese food, naturally enough, cooked specially for him by one or two of the Chinese restaurants in Chinatown. I remember how he would sit there eating this special food with all his students around him, holding court."

With his television career established - at least for the moment - it wasn't long after his arrival in Los Angeles that Lee's thoughts turned to seriously resuming his martial arts career. After looking around the city for a suitable place, he opened a Kung Fu school in Chinatown. His arrival, according to Maydole, caused quite an uproar. "Nobody had ever taught Kung-Fu here before. Several top Karate black belts such as Danny Inosanto went over to Bruce and there was a lot of jealousy among the Karate people who said that Kung-Fu didn't mean anything. Bruce challenged them on several occasions, but nothing ever came of it. I suppose they knew in their hearts how good he was."

As their friendship developed, Maydole made a point of dropping in to Lee's new school where he picked up a few fragments of instruction. However, the photographer was sceptical as to the possible violent practical potential of Kung-Fu. Although he had studied judo in the Army, he was reluctant to commit himself too deeply to Kung-Fu. Judo was designed to ward off an attacker, he felt, but to him Kung-Fu seemed designed primarily to kill people or cripple them for life - Lee's expertise in particular unnerved him. "Bruce had this big wooden dummy which he would use, and once he showed me 52 ways of kicking it. By kicking on a certain place you could blind a person, cripple him, kill him - whatever you chose. And Bruce, with his big toe, he could kick in any one of those 52 places. He was always wearing bare feet or ballet shoes so he could use his toe more freely. His big toe was a lethal weapon. He could tick you with it on the chin from any direction without warning."

Although he never took up Kung-Fu, Maydole was immensely impressed by Lee's many deadly skills. He decided these movements would look good on film, and the photographs

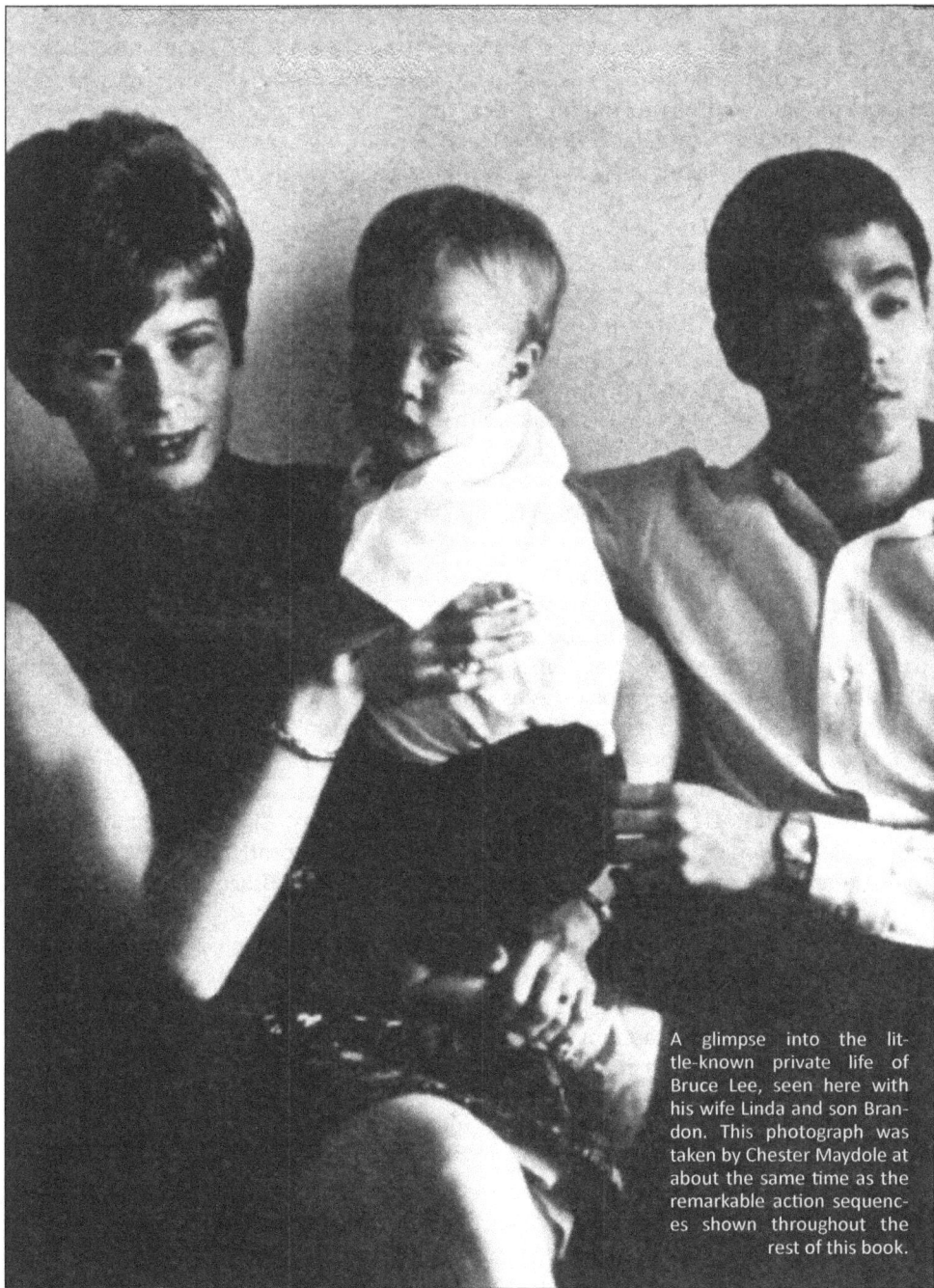

A glimpse into the little-known private life of Bruce Lee, seen here with his wife Linda and son Brandon. This photograph was taken by Chester Maydole at about the same time as the remarkable action sequences shown throughout the rest of this book.

in this book are the result. They were taken, recalls Maydole, "Just for the hell of it." He thought that with a little pushing he could sell some of them to a Karate magazine, and so the first of four sessions was set up. On Malibu Beach, Lee and his pupil, Danny Inosanto, ran through a series of attacks and defences for Chester Maydole's camera.

These shots of Lee and Inosanto sparring together are the finest photographs ever to be taken of Bruce Lee in action. Dressed in his black uniform with the Yin-Yang symbol he adopted as his school's emblem, he demonstrates a wealth of techniques from stance through defence movements to attack. Together with their respective captions, these photographs should illuminate much of Lee's martial wisdom which has hitherto been limited to mere words.

The photographs taken in Lee's 20th-floor luxury Los Angeles apartment are, of course, less valuable to the martial arts student, although they do depict some of Lee's training methods and equipment, plus a section of his martial arts library and weapons collection. However, as a record of Lee the man, they offer a touching glimpse into a little-known private life.

"Bruce was very proud of his wife and young son Brandon," remembers Maydole. "His other child was born after we lost contact with each other. Linda was very quiet. She never said a word which made her rather hard to get to know. Maybe she had decided to take a backseat to Bruce because he was the star. She was a martial artist herself though. And Brandon should be very good at Kung-Fu when he grows up, too. Even at that age, he was learning."

As it turned out, Chester Maydole never did sell the photographs. Suddenly he found himself working flat out, and he simply never got around to it. His heavy business schedule not only forced him to forget about the pictures, but it also brought about the end of his friendship with Lee. Bruce kept pressing Maydole to meet with him to plan a book on Jeet Kune Do, using Chester's pictures as illustrations. Maydole, with assignments as far away as India, had to keep postponing the meeting. Eventually Lee stopped phoning.

"It was just circumstances," recalls Maydole sadly. "Both of us trying to make a living. And, of course, I'm really sorry I didn't do the book."

As for the photographs, they just lay there gathering dust. "I stuck them in my dead picture file and forgot about them," says Maydole. "Then recently my agent mentioned he was after pictures of Bruce Lee. I said I had lots of shots of Bruce doing Kung-Fu. And that was that."

So, a decade after they were taken, Chester Maydole's remarkable collection of photographs has finally been published. In order for the reader to fully understand and realize the value of these historic records, they are divided into twenty-five numbered sequences accompanied by detailed captions and a comprehensive text.

The first part of the text charts Lee's life and martial career, providing a record of his achievements and the influences that he incorporated into Jeet Kune Do. The second and final part of the text is a detailed analysis of Lee's own martial creation, Jeet Kune Do, culled from the written and taped source material that he left behind.

It was always Lee's great fear that his art would be twisted and distorted by imitators. Here, then, for the first time since his death, is Bruce Lee performing his own art for that art's sake. If Chester Maydole's photographic portraits in any way provide a clearer, less distorted view of Bruce Lee's revolutionary legacy, they will have been well worth the wait.

CHAPTER ONE
BRUCE LEE THE MARTIAL ARTIST

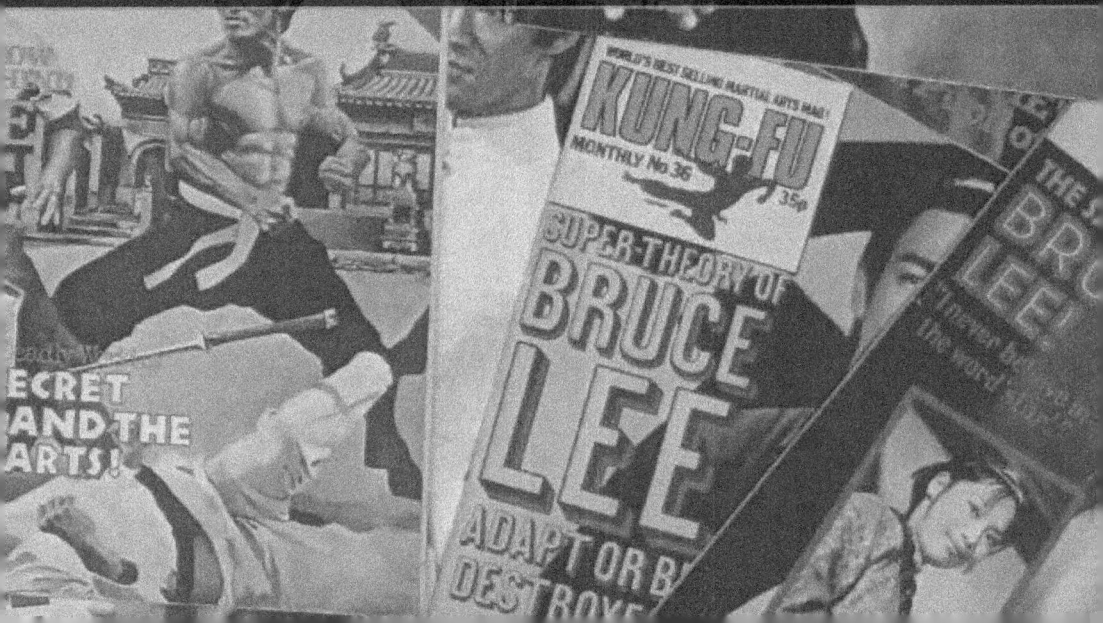

A learned man once asked a Zen teacher to instruct him. The teacher began to talk, but the learned man persisted in interrupting him, "Oh, yes, I know that already," and "That is of course a part of many philosophies." At last the Zen master stopped talking and prepared to serve the learned man tea. He filled up his cup and then kept on pouring until it overflowed. "Enough," exclaimed the learned man. "My cup is already full." "Indeed, so I see," said the teacher. "And if you do not empty your cup first, how can you expect to taste my tea?"

ANCIENT ZEN STORY

"The usefulness of the cup is in its emptiness."

BRUCE LEE

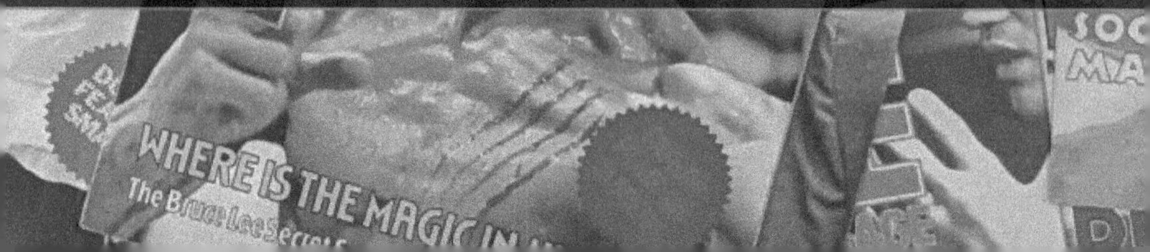

To understand the nature of Bruce Lee's martial legacy, it is necessary to examine the influences on the man throughout his life and martial career. Jeet Kune Do was a synthesis of myriad lessons Lee learned over the span of his short lifetime, and it is only after these influences are recognised that the student will be able to judge the full value of Jeet Kune Do. To do this we must travel back to Lee's earliest years.

STREET FIGHTER

Bruce Lee was born Li Yuen Kam - literally 'Protector of San Francisco' - on November 27, 1940, in San Francisco, half way around the world from his ancestors and origins. His parents - Li Hoi-chuen and his wife Grace were performers with the Cantonese Opera, a sort of Chinese vaudeville show, and they were in America on an extended tour of the country's crowded Chinatowns.

At the age of three, Lee returned with his parents to his native Hong Kong. His childhood was idyllic by any standard, let alone the prevailing standards of his teeming Asian homeland. His parents were well-off, Bruce had several brothers to play with, and he discovered that he was quick to make friends. More than that, by the age of six he had become a fledgling movie star. Although his first role was in a Cantonese tearjerker called The Birth of Mankind which even the most ardent film fan found ludicrous, Lee went on to make no less than seventeen more films, earning himself a reputation as a competent and skilful performer.

Lee was no ordinary boy and even the extraordinary diversions of a career in the Cantonese film world could not command his attention for long. By the time he had reached his teens, he had joined up with a gang of youths his own age and was deeply immersed in learning the language of the streets.

Street gangs are a phenomenon which occur in virtually every big, modern city, especially in centres of overcrowded, high-rise urban development. Hong Kong, like New York, has more than its share of this sort of juvenile activity. With family crowded on top of family for miles around, it is little wonder that boys group together to carve out their own 'territory,' battling for supremacy in the streets, back alleys and across the rooftops.

But street warfare in Hong Kong runs deeper than in most other cities - East or West. Street gangland is a testing ground for the criminals of the future in Hong Kong's notorious 'mafia' - the Triad Organization.

To succeed on the street means a membership card in this secret network, which has a finger in a huge assortment of crimes ranging from grassroots protection rackets to large-scale international drug smuggling. As an indication of the organisation's size and manpower strength, in 1975 the Hong Kong Police's Triad Society Bureau arrested more than eleven hundred suspected Triad members.

It was into this twilight world of organised juvenile crime that Lee leaped at the tender age of 13. Such were his single-mindedness and leadership abilities that within a very short space of time he had risen through the ranks of his gang and taken command.

"I was a punk," he told a martial arts magazine many years later, "and went looking for fights. We used chains and pens with knives hidden inside." On other occasions he wore a toilet chain wrapped around his waist, similar to the motorcycle chains carried by

Western youths.

"Bruce was a thug," admitted one of his close friends and business associates of later years. "He was a little villain."

The gangs were Lee's first introduction to combat and he learned their lessons well. They taught the boy alertness, speed and cunning. More importantly, they taught him a simple credo which Lee took to heart: winning is everything, style and rules count for nothing in combat. Lee soon learned that he was walking through a jungle where honour could prove to be a fatal liability and 'correct' combat techniques could be a fighter's downfall.

There were no Marquis of Queensbury rules on the street of Hong Kong; you fought to win at all costs. This was a lesson Lee would carry with him throughout his life. In time it would form the basis of his whole philosophy of martial combat.

Where Lee's gangland expertise would have led him had he continued on the streets is anyone's guess. He would most likely have either become a man of power, served a

Bruce Lee defends an attack with a left-handed outside block using the palm heel to the wrist or forearm. He follows up with a right straight-forward kick to the abdomen, the middle line or the groin. When his attacker retaliates, Lee immediately leaps in with a spear thrust to the neck or eyes

life-time in prison or died in some Kowloon back alley with a knife in his back. As he later admitted himself, life with the Triad Society was once a strong possibility for his future career.

Ironically enough, it was Lee's burning desire to rise to supremacy on the streets that eventually caused his break with the gangs. "One day I wondered what would happen if I didn't have a gang behind me if I got into a fight," he told an interviewer in 1967. "I decided to learn how to protect myself and I began to study Kung-Fu."

The martial arts are an integral part of the social fabric of Hong Kong. From youngsters to old men, the arts are practiced as a philosophy of life, a defence, a sport and as a means of keeping fit. From his childhood, Lee would have been exposed to the martial arts in one form or another. Indeed, Lee's actor father was one of the thousands of middle-aged and elderly men who crowd Hong Kong's parks and open spaces each weekend to run through the various set movements and disciplines of T'ai Chi-chuan in order to keep fit.

As seen in the previous section, T'ai Chi dates back 1,500 years to the Taoist monks. Its basis is its softness and slow movement which produce a balance between mind, body and spirit. Its movements are designed to exercise even the smallest joints and muscles of the body. This, in turn, stimulates the blood circulation and makes the body supple.

As a mental discipline, T'ai Chi provides a harmony of mind and body, thus generating the spiritual energy known as 'chi.' A source of power which in time Lee would come to know and to harness, Chi points the way to inner awareness, putting the disciple in touch with himself and his universe.

It is impossible to believe that Lee's father did not pass on to his young son some of the truths of T'ai Chi. Certainly many of its precepts appeared in Lee's later philosophy. But as a teenager, Lee was more interested in finding a more effective way of despatching his young opponents, rather than consulting the universe. "What I was really interested in was self-defence," he remarked in one interview. "We Chinese have been developing and perfecting methods of armed and unarmed combat for thousands of years, and the study of martial arts is a venerable and respected one. It is also very handy if you happen to live in a tough neighbourhood like I did."

Although Lee initially discarded the gentle T'ai Chi, the art did open to him a glimpse of the potential of some of the more aggressive martial forms. Lee's initial step towards 'Kung-Fu' was undoubtedly the most impor-

Here we see the attacker moving forward with a right-handed attack, using a spear thrust to the middle of his opponent. This particular form of attack is countered by dropping the palm heel of the left hand and hooking the fingers around the attacking arm. Bruce Lee's counter-attacks can use either the right-footed straight kick, picture, or a right roundhouse kick, picture.

The final picture shows the follow-up, a knife hand thrust to the head or shoulders. This technique is equally useful against the face. When using this defence/counter-attack method, it is important, when hooking the left hand onto the attacker's arm, to pull the attacker towards you so as to throw him off balance while retaliating.

tant decision he was to make in his life, even though at the time he seized it merely as a means to a not-so-honourable end.

STUDENT FIGHTER

When Lee decided to investigate Kung-Fu, his knowledge of the martial arts was, at best, minimal and, like so many Western youngsters of today anxious to uncover mysterious and mystical truths, he was ripe for exploitation. Fortunately for him he chose as his school the Wing Chun style of Kung-Fu and as his master an old man named Ip Man. Ip Man had brought the secrets of Wing Chun from behind the bamboo curtain when he fled mainland China. In Hong Kong he established himself as Wing Chun's greatest modern practitioner. The Wing Chun school had been founded sometime between the 16th and 17th centuries by Madame Yim Wing Chun (literally, Beautiful Springtime). It originated, according to popular belief, from the division between hard and soft Kung-Fu systems.

While studying martial art under a Shaolin nun, Ng Mui, Yim Wing Chun became disillusioned by both the inordinately elaborate set moves and the emphasis on aggression and brute strength of the Shaolin system. Determined to overcome what she saw as defects, she developed a new, close-quarter system by reducing the number of 'sets' or 'katas' to just three.

The style that filtered down to Ip Man six generations later was this 'soft' cut-down version of Shaolin teaching, which attempted to harness an opponent's strength rather than trying to dominate it. Unhampered by unnecessary moves, and taking his or her cue from the opponent, the Wing Chun disciple is, after perfecting the style, able to fight and defend even while blindfolded.

Ip Man was a master of Wing Chun. But more than that, he was a realist, ever adapting his ideas to the changing world about him. Stripped of any unnecessary moves, Wing Chun was - and still is - one of the most adaptable Kung-Fu schools, and under Ip Man's guidance, the style was subtly altered to deal with the changing patterns of modern life. In particular, Ip Man strove to teach swift, sudden attack and close, riskless defence.

For Bruce Lee the gang-leader, Wing Chun was a powerful weapon which he found could be used to great advantage in his twilight world on the crowded streets. Lee took to his new discovery like a duck to water. In order to toughen his fists he would bang the side of his hand against the leg of his stool between bites at mealtimes. Sometimes, jealous of his fellow students, he would stand outside the school door telling his colleagues, "No class today." Then, when they had returned home, he would enter and gain the benefits of a sole student under Ip Man.

Although Kung-Fu was, even then, something of a fad among members of the juvenile street gangs, the youths who stuck at the rigorous training schedules and demanding classes were few and far between. Lee's enthusiasm, on the other hand, was boundless, and gradually Wing Chun took over his life.

Kung-Fu did not change Lee's life immediately. For years he still regarded it as just another weapon in his street arsenal, albeit a weapon which he spent long, arduous hours perfecting. In his early martial days he would often leave Ip Man's classroom and stalk the back alleys looking for someone on whom to test what he had just learned.

One notorious - although probably exaggerated - example of his use of Kung-Fu was his high-rise battle against a rival gang-leader who had issued a challenge to duel. Lee's opponent chose the location and the rules, saying "We'll fight on a rooftop and the winner can toss the loser over." Lee consented and the two squared off on the roof of a five-storey Kowloon apartment block. As Lee was removing his jacket, his antagonist savagely kicked

Following on from the previous sequence, the attacker has moved forward with a right-hand attack. A block with the left hand throws him off-balance. The defender then ducks inside the attacking hand and uses his own palm heel to attack the groin. The defender then grabs the attacker's hand with his own right hand, and counter-attacks by the use of a hammer fist to the attacker's head. Lee then launches into s a further counter-attacking measure using the palm heel on the back of the neck.

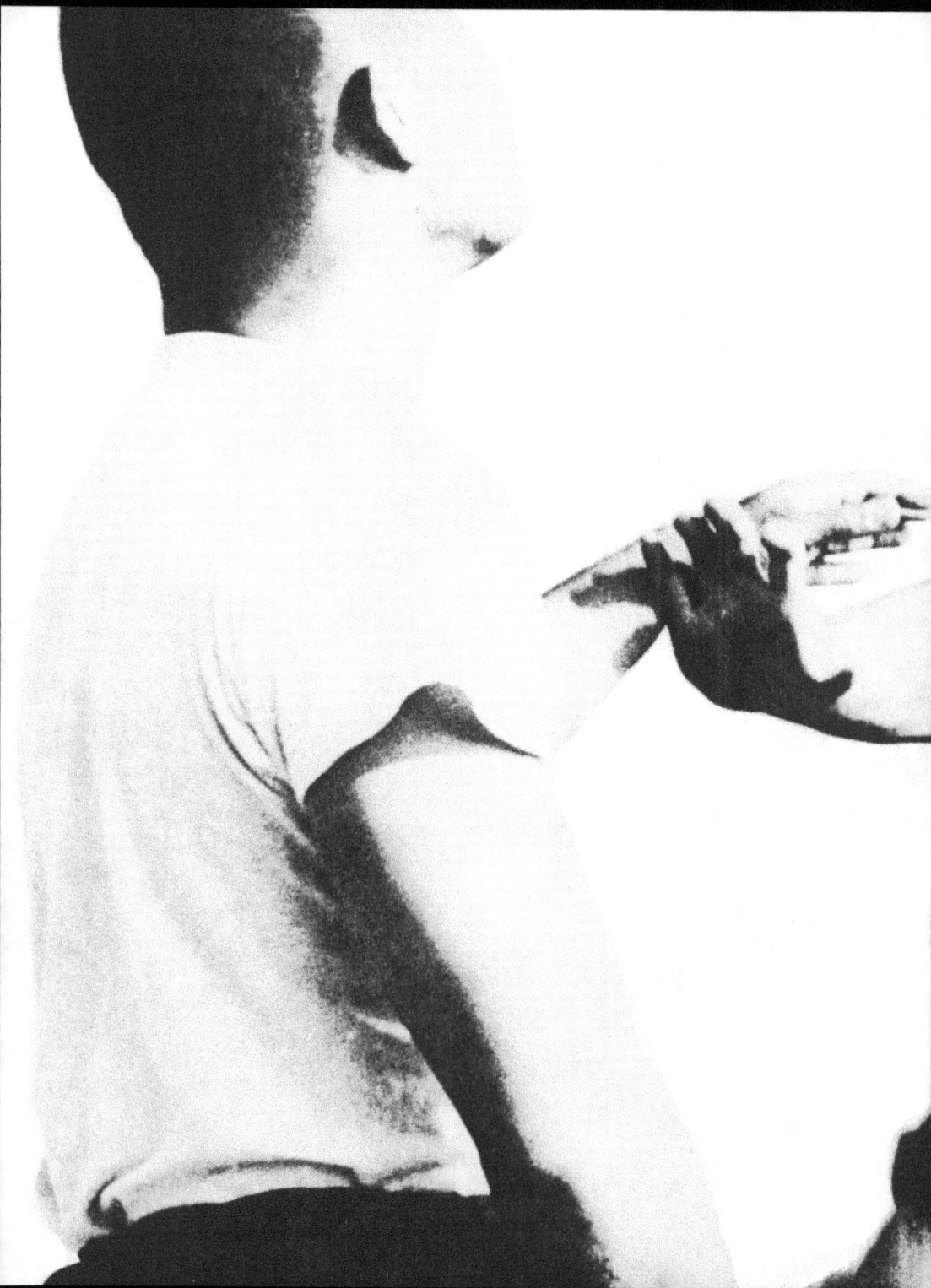

This time Bruce is attacked with a left-handed thrust. He defends with the right hand which uses the knife hand block against the inside edge of the attacking arm. At once he is able to counter-attack with a right roundhouse kick or a side kick to the stomach, face or groin.

Within three years Lee had become more than just adept at Wing Chun; he was a star pupil. The energy which he had used on the streets was now channelled into tuition. The aggression and cockiness was still there, but instead of being turned into senseless violence, it became a spur to his learning.

Traditionally, Kung-Fu schools play out ritual clashes among themselves, testing their systems against the systems of other martial artists. (A good example of the traditional 'animosity' is seen in Lee's film Fist of Fury, in which the rival Japanese school takes on Lee's Kung-Fu school.) Such stand-offs were a welcome outlet for Lee's aggression.

"Like the old tradition, one school would challenge another" he told one interviewer, "and a designated place and time would be set. On the day of reckoning, both schools would have their instructors and students to cheer their fighter. Impromptu rules would be established, but those rules would be so minimal that the fight would be just about 'all out'. Nobody really got hurt because the arts weren't all that effective. Those guys would have torn shirts and bloody noses, but I never saw anybody really get hurt badly enough to be sent to the hospital."

Lee could not bear to be bested in such tournaments. One example of his determination occurred when he and some other new students became the butt of the older students' ridicule. "Those bastards enjoyed overpowering us," he recalled, "and as we weakened they used to slap us on our chest and face. I got so mad one day that I decided to dish out the same medicine to them. I made a concentrated effort to develop my flowing energy. While attending class, I began to press my arm at the edge of the desk and flowed my energy.

One of the friendlier senior students spent some time after workouts exercising with me. In a few months I got my revenge, and did I dish it out to them! I really picked on them after that."

Another example of just how good Lee had become by his mid-teens can be seen by the way in which he despatched a rival High School boxing champion. One of Lee's old masters, Brother Edward of the Saint Francis Xavier College, remembered the incident. "When he came to our school I knew at once he was a boxer," Brother Edward remembers. "He was already that good. We once had a boxing match at the rival St. George's school and, although Bruce didn't know much about European boxing, he challenged their champion."

Lee also remembered the incident. "I hadn't any training in boxing, but decided to enter because I thought I was pretty good in Wing Chun and there wouldn't be much difference between my art and boxing. I never put on a glove before, and it sure felt funny when I got into the ring. I learned to hit straight forward in Wing Chun, and that's what I did, knocking down my opponent."

A PHILOSOPHY OF FIGHTING

While Lee's physical skills multiplied at an astonishing rate and his once-scrawny body filled out into a powerful tool, for the first four years of his training the spiritual aspects of the young fighter.

Lee knew that Kung-Fu was more than just a physical exercise: It is a subtle art ot

The attacker tries a right-handed punch to Bruce Lee's head. Lee defends with an outside block using the palm heel of his left hand. Immediately he ducks under the attacker's blow to counter-attack with a back-handed blow from the knuckles of his left hand. The final picture shows how a left-handed punch to the mid-section can be used if any further counter-attack is needed.

matching the essence of the mind to that of the technique in which it has to work," as he would later write. However, he could not grow to oneness with the Universe, nor could he capture and hold the inherent gentleness of Kung-Fu, Wing Chun in particular. After four years of practice, he could understand the idea of gentleness and the concept of following an opponent's movements, riding on his energy with the minimum output of one's own aggression. However, in combat his ability to capture this gentleness vanished and he found himself and again filled with the desire to overpower his opponent.

Ip Man tried to instil in his pupil the ability to relax and detach himself so as to be capable of flowing with the movement of the aggressor. "Preserve yourself by following the natural bends of things and don't interfere," the old man counselled. "Remember never to assert yourself against nature: never be in frontal opposition to any problems, but learn to control it by swinging with it."

One day, Ip Man ordered Lee not to practice for a week but to go home and think about the gentleness he could not cultivate. What resulted was the subject of a College essay Lee later wrote, recorded by his wife in her book Bruce Lee: The Man Only I Knew. "The following week I stayed home," wrote Lee. "After spending many hours in meditation and practice, I gave up and went sailing alone in a junk. On the sea, I thought of all my past training and got mad at myself and punched at the water. Right then at that moment, a thought suddenly struck me. Wasn't this water, the very basic stuff, the essence of Kung-Fu? Didn't the common water just illustrate to me the principle of Kung-Fu? I struck it just now, but it did not suffer hurt. Again I stabbed it with all my might, yet it was not wounded. I then tried to grasp a handful of it but it was impossible. This water, the softest substance in the world, could fit itself into any container. Although it seemed weak, it could penetrate the hardest substance in the world. That was it! I wanted to be like the nature of water."

"Suddenly a bird flew past and cast its reflection on the water. Right then, as I was absorbing myself, another mystic sense of hidden meaning started upon me. Shouldn't it be the same then that the thoughts and emotions I had in front of an opponent passed like the reflection of the bird over the water? This was exactly what Professor Ip meant by being detached - not being without emotion or feeling, but being one in whom feeling was not sticky or blocked. Therefore in order to control myself I must first accept myself by going with, and not against, my nature."

Lee lay back in the boat, letting it drift where it would. He had discovered in himself the essence of a spirituality sought after by martial artists for thousands of years. From that moment, Kung-Fu for Lee would never again be just a way of beating up opponents. In the coming years he would pursue spirituality and philosophy as avidly as he would develop his physical ability.

I know he caused his parents terrible heartache and sleepless nights," said Lee's wife, Linda, at a later date. "They knew he was out prowling the streets at night. I think his wild prowling was the reason for his parents sending him back to America."

A NEW LAND

In late 1958, Lee, with one hundred dollars in his pocket, booked a passage on a cheap freighter and headed for America. He landed in the city of his birth - San Francisco's Chinatown. After a few months of living with friends of his parents and earning his keep teaching dance lessons (Lee had once been the Cha Cha champion of Hong Kong), he travelled north to Seattle where he be-

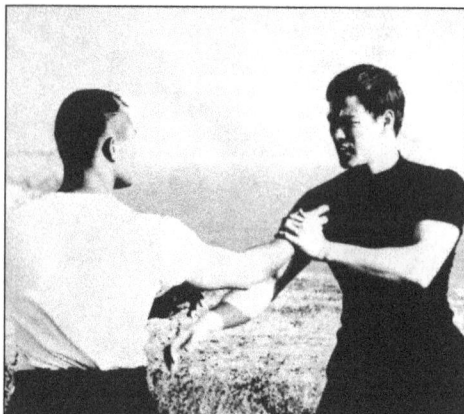

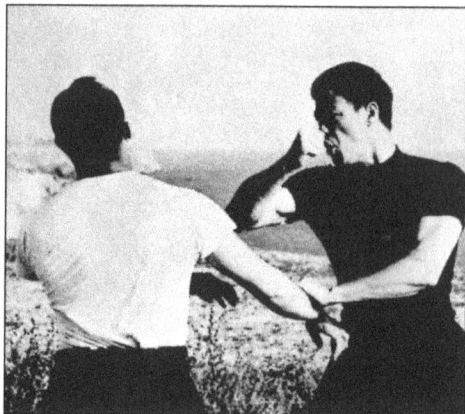

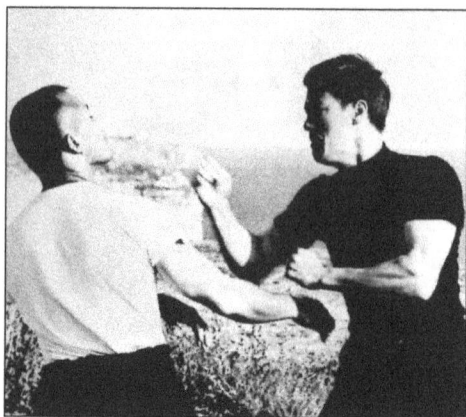

The attack this time comes from the right hand. Lee defends with a block and track, with his left hand hooking the palm heel and fingers onto his opponent's arm. He counter-attacks simultaneously with a back-hand blow to the face. In this case he uses the inverted fist and its first two knuckles for the blow.

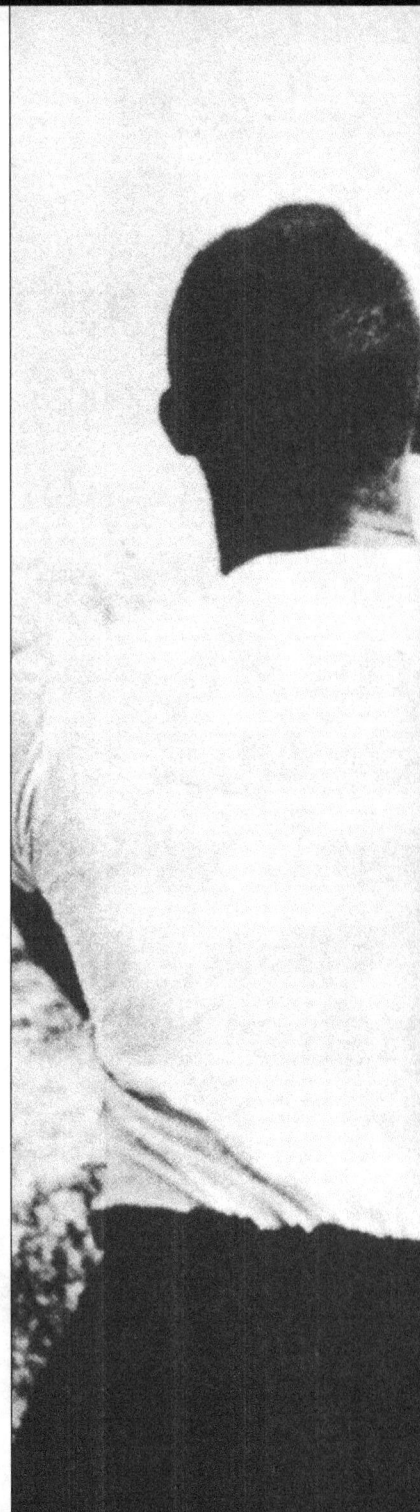

Another left-handed attack is averted as Bruce uses his block and track technique, pulling forward with the left hand to keep his attacker off balance. Once again his counter-attack is launched with a back-handed blow from the inverted fist. This time he follows up at once, with a spear-thrust at the eyes. It is important here to remember to keep hold of the attacker's arm and pull him forward, thus ensuring his continued lack of balance throughout.

came a dishwasher and waiter in a Chinese restaurant owned by a local figure, Ruby Chow. Ruby, a friend of the family, looked after the youth, making sure he settled into his new environment.

Lee enrolled at Seattle's Edison Technical High School, studying hard and improving his English and mathematics after the last customer had gone home. Besides his job and his studies, Lee also kept up his Kung-Fu, practicing every day against a piece of padded board he hung in Ruby Chow's kitchen.

Eventually the studies paid off. Lee graduated from Edison and enrolled at Seattle's Washington University, majoring in philosophy. His constant Kung-Fu practice also paid dividends, so much so that he was soon able to quit the restaurant and earn a living teaching the martial arts. Ever since his arrival in America he had wanted to start his own school, but he was afraid that the time it would consume would detract too much from his studies.

Lee's first 'school' was in fact little more than a collection of people grouped together in a park or parking lot. He was still too impoverished to afford to rent premises. There in the open, Lee would run through the precepts of Kung-Fu, stressing fluidity and the harmony between the inner spirit and the physical action. All that he had learned from Ip Man he tried to impart on his followers. He would illustrate his lessons with the most amazing movements, far in advance of anything anyone in America had ever seen. Even the most experienced Kung-Fu devotees were astounded.

Linda Lee records Taky Kimura's first encounter with Lee back in 1959. Kimura, who would later become Lee's most devoted follower, had taken up the martial arts to try and gain self-confidence, but all he had been able to find were various methods of body-building. One day some of his friends came and told him about a new guy fresh from Hong Kong who could perform incredible feats. Without putting too much store by these claims, Kimura sought out Lee on the University campus where he was practising on the football field. "I was so amazed and impressed with his ability that I immediately asked if I could join his club." remembers Kimura, "For almost a year, we just met in parks on Sundays. I was intrigued by his tremendous power, of being light one minute and really deep the next."

As Lee's skills improved, so too did his physique develop in the United States. He became conscious of his health and began to eat beneficial food and concentrate more on physical exercise. He also began taking large doses of vitamins and going for long, early-morning runs over rough and hilly terrain. In the campus gymnasium he became entranced by weight-lifting, working out with large weights and with small single-hand dumbbells. But it was not large and bulky muscles that Lee was striving for. Rather, he was attempting to build and strengthen every joint and muscle in his body, no matter how small.

It was not long before Lee's remarkable prowess became famous among Kung-Fu students. After marrying a fellow student from the University - Linda - he abandoned his philosophy course and opened up a school in a small Seattle basement. He called his school the Jun Fan Kung-Fu Institute - 'Bruce Lee's Kung-Fu Institute.' His fee at that time was just $15 for a month's instruction!

Soon after, Lee and his young bride returned to California and settled in Oakland, just across the bay from San Francisco. He left the running of the Seattle school in the hands

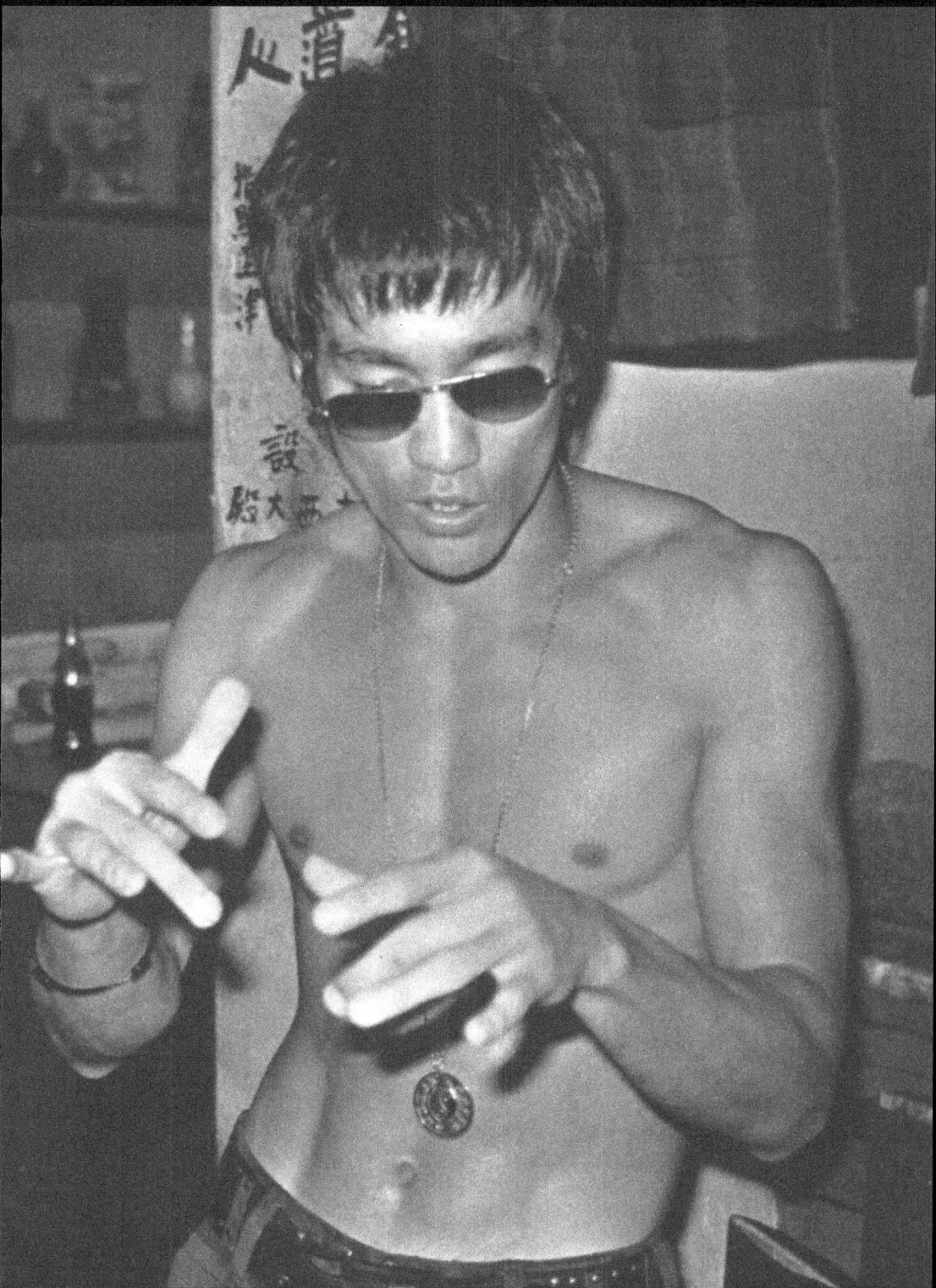

of his friend Taky Kimura. In Oakland, Lee, together with another colleague of his, James Lee, opened a second Jun Fan Institute.

Kung-Fu was one art the Chinese knew was solely their own, and they guarded its secrets jealously. For centuries, the Chinese people had been oppressed and made to feel inferior to other races and nations. Waves of foreigners - especially the hated Japanese - had humiliated the Chinese through conquest. Kung-Fu was a way in which the Chinese could be made to feel superior to other races. Like the secret societies of the Boxer era, Chinese exponents of Kung-Fu followed an unwritten code which forbade them passing on the secrets of the art to non-Chinese.

But Bruce Lee was no ordinary Kung-Fu teacher. He did not believe Kung-Fu was the sole property of one race; Kung-Fu, he reasoned, belonged to anyone who wished to take up its calling. It was not that Lee was blind to the potential of Kung-Fu for the Chinese race - in later years he would make a film - Fist of Fury - in which the hero would wipe out a treacherous Karate school, shouting in the faces of his vanquished opponents, "We are no longer sick men of Asia."

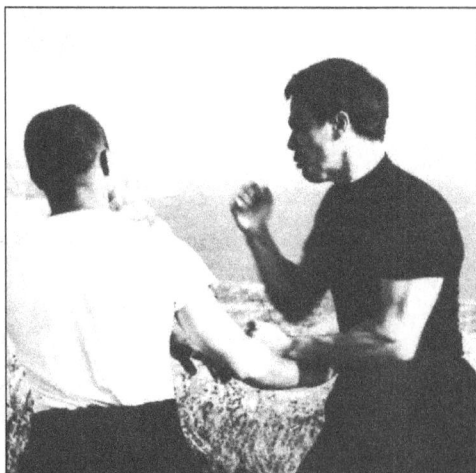

However, Lee believed that if someone came to him seriously seeking knowledge, race or colour was of little importance. Through his instruction and later, through his films, Lee could reasonably be judged the 'father' of modern Kung-Fu. Almost single-handedly he brought the art to a dozen nations and made it a household name around the globe.

Back in San Francisco, however, Lee was an unpopular man amongst the Chinese Kung-Fu community for his determination to teach Westerners his skills. Soon after he had established his kwoon - or school - on San Francisco's Broadway, Lee was paid a visit by the top local Kung-Fu practitioner, a young Chinese recently arrived from Hong Kong.

Supported by several of his colleagues, this young man challenged Lee to a duel, implying that if Lee lost he would have to close down his kwoon Incensed, Lee decided to establish his credentials once and for all. In so doing, he showed just how skilled he had become. Within a minute, San Francisco's champion had turned tail and fled!

Lee continued to teach Wing Chun for several years. Soon he had perfected everything Ip Man had taught him and he began to feel the restrictions of style. Although Madam Wing Chun had devised he method as a system virtually without set patterns, it was still a system nonetheless. Over the years Lee had come to recognise not only the rigidity of style, but also its dangers.

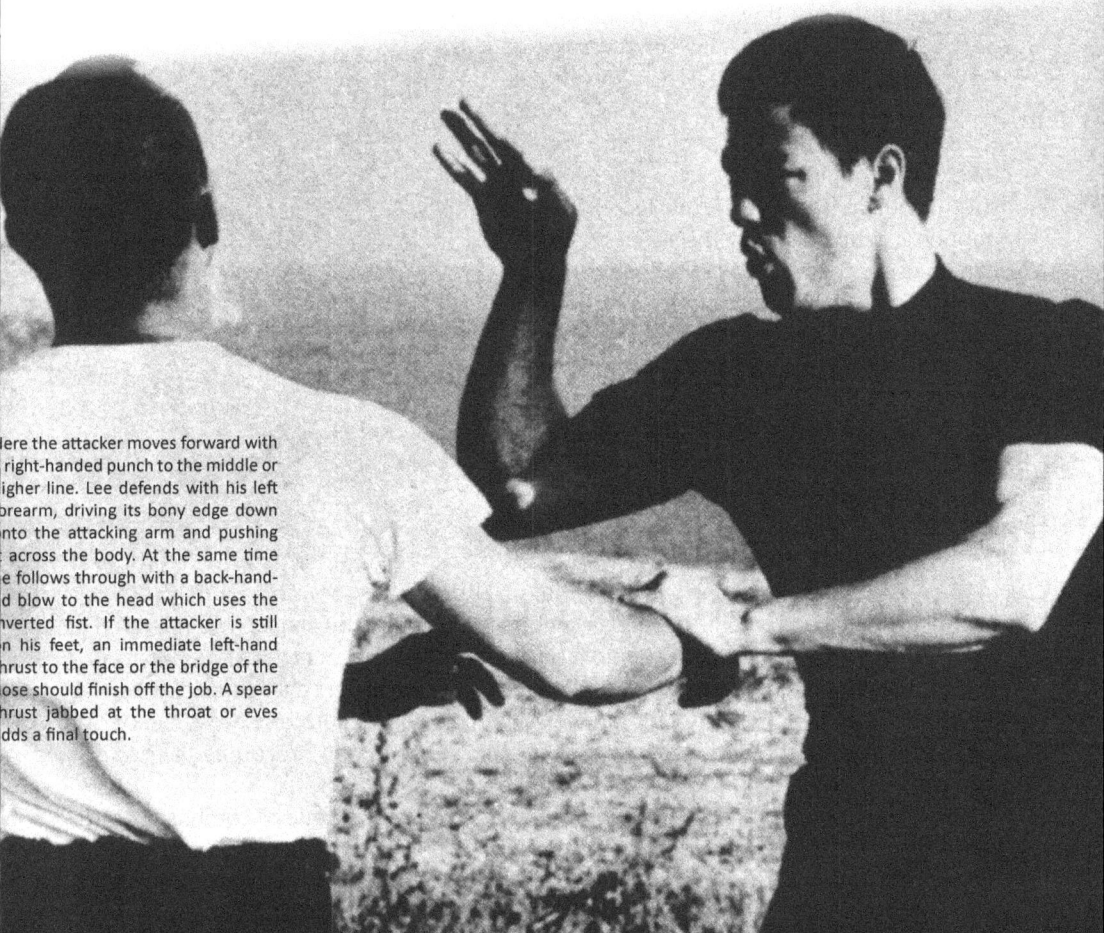

Here the attacker moves forward with a right-handed punch to the middle or higher line. Lee defends with his left forearm, driving its bony edge down into the attacking arm and pushing it across the body. At the same time he follows through with a back-hand-ed blow to the head which uses the inverted fist. If the attacker is still on his feet, an immediate left-hand thrust to the face or the bridge of the nose should finish off the job. A spear thrust jabbed at the throat or eyes adds a final touch.

A NEW STYLE

"I saw the limitations in Wing Chun," Lee once told an interviewer from Black Belt Magazine. "I'd gotten into a fight in San Francisco with a Kung-Fu cat, and after a brief encounter the son-of-a-bitch started to run. I chased him and, like a fool, kept punching him behind his head and back. Soon my fists began to swell from hitting his hard head. Right then I realised Wing Chun was not too practical and began to alter my way of fighting."

The way Lee began changing his style was simple; he literally threw everything he had ever learned into his combat. Like Ip Man, he realised Kung-Fu had to be practical to survive. It was no good to be a perfect master at performing sets - katas - no use at all, if you were beaten every time you faced a challenge.

Lee had boundless respect for the various forms of fighting (Karate, Judo and so on), but he laughed in the face of an opponent who followed the rules at the risk of losing chances. To be bogged down by form was not merely an error to Lee, it was a deadly sin. Outside his school he erected a small gravestone with the pithy epitaph; "In Memory of a Once Fluid Man Crammed and Distorted by the Classical Mess." To rely on classical forms and katas was, to Lee, like fighting with an arm in plaster.

"While I was a student at the university," Lee once recounted, "I gave a demonstration of Kung-Fu. While explaining the art is the forerunner of Karate, I was rudely interrupted by a black belt Karateman from Japan who sat in front of the stage. "No, no, Karate not from China. Come from Japan!" he hollered. Lee replied that in fact, Karate had its origins in Kung-Fu. After the audience had filed out, the Karate expert challenged Lee to a fight. "Anytime," said Lee. "Okay, I fight you next week," said the Karateman. "Why not now?" suggested Lee. "It only took me two seconds to dispose of him," recounted Lee later. "He was too slow and too stiff!"

Building on his basis of Wing Chun, Lee added code after code of combat styles to his repertoire. His library was enormous, shelf upon shelf filled with hundreds of books on every conceivable form of self-defence - Western boxing, Thai kick boxing, French box-

The next three sequences of pictures show ways of using the nunchakus both for defence and then immediately as a means of counter-attack. This potent weapon consists simply of three sturdy sticks joined at two points by a chain some six inches long.

This attack comes with a thrust of the spear to Lee's stomach and body. Ready for defence, Lee holds the outside pole of the nunchakus in his left hand, while the middle section is grasped in his right one. He defends by using his right hand to smash the outside stick of the weapon onto the spear, thus deflecting it, while at the same time he moves into attack by flicking the other outside nunchaku stick through a full 180° to crack home, beneath his opponent's chin.

In this sequence, as the attacker moves forward, thrusting the spear at Lee's head and body, the three-section staff held ready in both hands. It shows how Lee can deflect the attacker's spear with his left-hand stick. The right-hand stick comes into action as the spear carrier attempts to swing his weapon back into the defender's face. Bruce Lee counter-attacks after avoiding the spear thrust by using a side snap-kick to the attacker's forward spear-holding hand, thus loosening his grip and preparing him for further punishment.

ing, judo, karate, wrestling and so on. To this he added all the tricks and sly feints he had learned on the streets of Hong Kong - the raw, naked, aggressive, lawless tactics never seen in a gymnasium, let alone taught.

He was determined to master an art which permitted him to respond naturally to every move of his opponent, no matter what his enemy threw at him. Also, he strove to become the master of surprise himself, being able to slide through an opponent's set, memorized defences like a knife through butter.

A friend of Lee's, Adrian Marshall, tells a similar story. While sparring, Marshall found that fighting with Lee was like butting a brick wall. "Bruce tied me up like a pretzel so that I couldn't move," he recalls. "I stood there, totally frustrated - whatever I tried, Bruce could counter it with ease. Try something else,' commanded Bruce. 'What?' I shouted angrily. 'What can I do?' 'You could always bite,' laughed Bruce. But he meant it. In one of his films, the villain ties him up - in a wrestling hold. So what does he do? - he bites!"

"Bruce was creative and original," said his close friend and fellow instructor Dan Inosanto after Lee's death. "He advanced in the martial arts because he dared to question the principles that were laid as rules, or foundations. Bruce said,

"There is no rule that has been set down that cannot be broken. It might have been functional at one time, but it may not be functional today."

This was the essence of Lee's thought and he turned it into a system which was, in fact, no style at all. "I personally don't believe in the word style," Lee told Hong Kong broadcaster Ted Thomas. "Not unless there are human beings with three arms and four legs, unless we have another group of human beings structurally different from us, then there might be a different style of fighting.

"The unfortunate thing is that there's boxing which uses hands, judo which is throwing and so on, I am not putting any of these down, but what I am saying is that because of styles people are separated. They are not united because styles become law. The original founder starts off with hypotheses, but then they become the gospel truth. When you use a Japanese style, then you are expressing a Japanese style, not yourself. You must ask yourself, 'How can I honestly express myself?' At the moment you punch, you must really be in that punch."

"I am no style, but I am all styles," Lee would tell his pupils. "You don't know what I am going to do, and even I don't know what I am going to do. My movement is the result of your movement; my technique

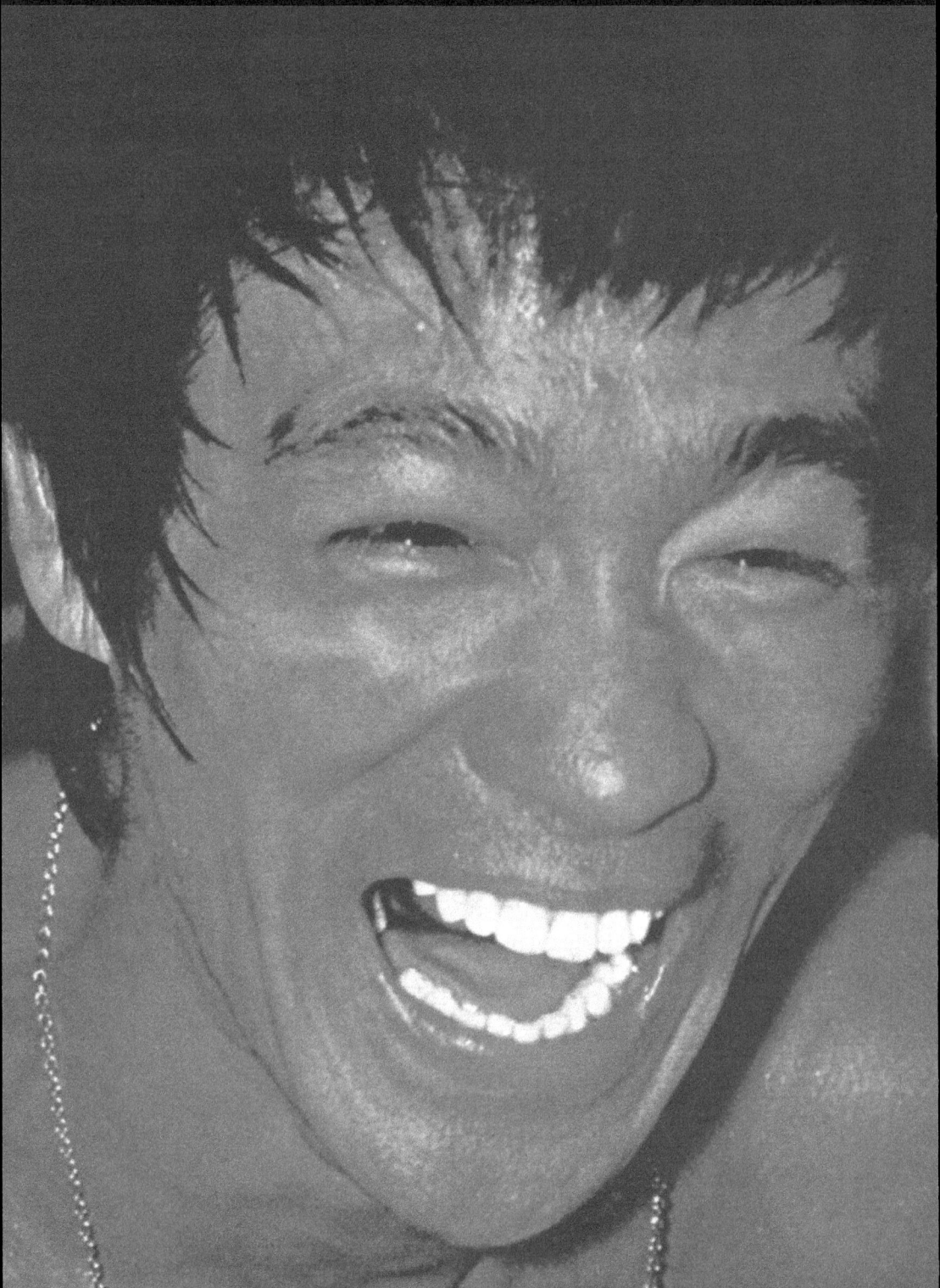

CHAPTER TWO
JEET KUNE DO

"For security, the unlimited living is turned into something dead, a chosen pattern that limits. To understand Jeet Kune Do, one ought to throw away all ideals, patterns, styles; in fact, one should throw away even the concepts of what is or isn't ideal in Jeet Kune Do. Can you look at a situation without naming it? Naming it, making it a word, causes fear."

BRUCE LEE, *TAO OF JEET KUNE DO*

"Let it be understood once and for all that I have not invented a new style, composite or modification," Lee told the readers of Black Belt Magazine in 1971. "I have in no way set Jeet Kune Do within a distinct form governed by laws that distinguish it from 'this' style or 'that' method. On the contrary, I hope to free my comrades from bondage to styles, patterns and doctrines."

UNDERSTANDING JEET KUNE DO

What Lee was striving to formulate with Jeet Kune Do was a universal style, a method by which any fighter could face another on equal terms regardless of background. It was as he would often remark, "a sophisticated form of street fighting." That is, the rules were only what the individual decided they were. To achieve this, meant jettisoning all restrictions, which meant that the keynote of Jeet Kune Do became simplicity.

"In building a statue," Lee taught, "a sculptor doesn't keep adding clay to his subject. Actually, he keeps chiselling away at the inessentials until the truth is revealed without obstructions. Jeet Kune Do doesn't mean adding more. It means to minimize. In other words, to hack away the inessentials. It is not a "daily increase,' but a 'daily decrease.' Art is really the expression of the self. The more complicated and restricted the method, the less the opportunity for the expression of one's original sense of freedom.

"Though they play an important role in the early stage, the techniques should not be too mechanical, complex or restrictive. If we cling blindly to them, we will eventually become bound by their limitations. Remember, you are expressing the techniques and not doing the techniques. If somebody attacks you, your response is not Technique No. 1, Stance No. 2, Section 4, Paragraph 5. Instead, you simply move in like sound and echo, without deliberation."

Lee graphically illustrated this point to a reporter who asked him what he meant by 'directness' in his lessons. In a flash, Lee's wallet was flying across the room to the startled reporter who, with a reflex action, caught it. "That," laughed Lee, "is directness. You did what comes naturally. You didn't waste time. You just reached up and caught the wallet - and you didn't squat, grunt or go into a horse stance or embark on some such classical move before reaching out for the wallet. You wouldn't have caught it if you had."

Simplicity Lee defined as absolute mastery. "Before I studied the art, a punch to me was just like a punch, a kick just like a kick. After I'd first learned the art, a punch was no longer a punch, a kick no longer a kick. Now that I've understood the art, a punch is just like a punch, a kick just like a kick."

"The height of cultivation is nothing special. It is mere simplicity, the ability to express the utmost with the minimum. It is the halfway cultivation that leads to ornamentation."

Of course, as Lee himself discovered as a boy under the instruction of Ip Man, to understand something - gentleness, simplicity or whatever - and be able to live that which you understand are two different things. To teach simplicity was far from easy, even when it seemed so obvious. On more than one occasion, Lee would use an anecdote to illustrate the heart of Jeet Kune Do: "Two Orientals were watching the Olympic Games in Rome. One of the chief attractions was Bob Hayes, the sprinter, in the hundred yards. As the gun went off, the spectators leaned forward in their seats, tense with excitement. With the runners reaching their goal, Hayes forged ahead and flashed across the line, the winner with a new world record of 9.1 seconds. As the crowd cheered, one of the Orientals elbowed the other in the ribs and said, 'Did you see that? His heel was too high up!"

All of which goes to provide a warning for any martial artist studying either the words of Bruce Lee or the pictures contained in this book. During his lifetime, Lee was terrified that somebody somewhere would take his words and turn them into a religion or a style that would bind future martial artists in a straight-jacket of second-hand wisdom. Because of this fear, Lee refused to publish his book, the Tao of Jeet Kune Do. Similarly he refused to open a chain of 'Jeet Kune Do' gymnasiums, although he would certainly have had little difficulty in finding backers.

"He didn't want to open a commercial school," remembered his co-instructor Dan Inosanto. "This is one of the promises that I made to him - that I would never open up a commercial school under the name Jeet Kune Do. He said, 'You could probably make some money out of it. But I'd be very disappointed if you did.'"

It is with these words in mind that the martial arts student should approach any instruction, either visual, written or physical, about Jeet Kune Do. If this instruction was to in any way hamper a student's individuality, cordoning him off from his own natural reactions, then it would be flying directly in the face of what Lee strove in the latter part of his martial career to promote. As usual, Lee himself said it best. After a short article

Another example of three-section staff use is demonstrated by Bruce. Here the weapon is seen in its long-range potential. As the attacker attempts to move forward and under Lee's guard, the staff is swung around through an arc of 180° and thus brings the end pole into play at great distance to threaten the attacker's head.

he contributed to the September 1971 issue of Black Belt Magazine outlining some of the philosophy behind Jeet Kune Do, he concluded by begging the reader to take his words, at best, as "a finger pointing to the moon."

"Please do not take the finger to be the moon," he wrote, using the imagery he so vividly incorporated into his philosophy, "or fix your gaze so intently on the finger as to miss all the beautiful sights of heaven. After all, the usefulness of the finger is in pointing away from itself to the light which illumines finger and all."

TRAINING

Lee's obsession with physical fitness is legendary. As a youth he was skinny and small and his physique was a source of endless embarrassment to him. Through Kung-Fu he discovered that he could build his body into a remarkable precision machine. It was an opportunity Lee grasped with both hands, and never let go.

Physical fitness became an integral part of Lee's life and he was short-tempered with anyone too lazy or ignorant to pursue it to the fullest. When Lee's brother Robert visited the United States, Lee met him at the airport. When they came face to face. Lee recoiled in horror. "Jesus you're skinny!" he exclaimed. "Don't tell anyone you're my brother - you'll embarrass me!"

Lee whisked his brother home and early next morning shook him awake and sent him out on a three mile run. He also concocted what he considered to be a suitable diet for his brother.

"Boy, that was really torture," remembers Robert. "Bruce was like a drill sergeant. He'd mix it every day himself to make sure I'd drink it. It had milk, quick-weight-gain protein powder, banana, ice-cream, egg shells and peanut butter. He made me drink a quart everyday!"

This attack comes from a right-handed blow. The defender uses his palm heel thrust down onto the attacker's wrist or forearm with the full force of his left arm. He hooks onto the attacking wrist and retaliates with a right-hand straight kick to the body or solar plexus. Also shown is a variation on this counter-attack, the side snap-kick to the neck. In the final picture of this sequence, Bruce performs yet another variation of retaliation by lifting his knee up to his chest with a bent leg, then stamping straight out to connect with his heel against the opposing chin.

Lee's own diet reflected his obsession with health, not entirely for the best, one can't help feeling. Often the food he ate seemed more as if he was attempting to mortify his taste buds, like some sort of ascetic monk, rather than provide himself with maximum nutrition. Often he went for long stretches living on just milk, eggs and raw beef mixed up together in a blender. On one occasion he was reported to be surviving on a novel diet of steak and cow's blood. In addition he would regularly gobble handfuls of vitamin pills. Perhaps the greatest benefit he derived from all of this bizarre consumption was that it kept him well away from alcohol, tobacco and restaurant food.

Although Lee kept an eagle eye on diet, exercise was the keystone of his training schedule. Before each training session he would run through a careful programme of warm-up exercises. "Warm-up exercises are a vital part of Kung-Fu training," he taught. "The muscles of the body are susceptible to injuries when they are not thoroughly warmed-up and limber." Lee stressed that the rise in body temperature after a warm-up helped allay muscle stiffness and soreness. Leg muscles in particular should be well exercised before a training session, he wrote.

This sequence shows Bruce demonstrating a simple kata (line form) using the nunchakus (fighting sticks; literally 'rice flail'). The nunchakus are always held in the right hand and Lee uses the chain to block any possible attack from a stick or other weapon. The final picture illustrates the back-handed swing.

The attacker moves forward with a right-handed blow. The defence in this case is with a left-handed block and track. The counter-attack comes at once, when Lee draws back his right hand across his face and then uses it to deliver a blow with his inverted fist against his attacker's head. It is worth noting that simultaneous to his right-handed blow, Lee moves forward with his right foot. This combination of foot and hand in the same direction will certainly add to the overall effect of any blow. Bruce is still holding onto his attacker's right hand, but his own follow through with the right-hand is blocked in its turn. Still pulling his attacker off balance with the left hand, Bruce takes the advantage by withdrawing his own right hand from the block before the attacker can get hold of it. Bruce then delivers a second back-hand blow to the head, following up if necessary, with an elbow thrust to the head, neck or body.

Lee believed that every student should work out between visits to the gymnasium using a range of homemade devices and a set of simple exercises. Indeed, simplicity was the foundation of his whole regimen and he especially favoured basic, everyday techniques.

"To me the best exercise is running," he told Black Belt Magazine. "Running is so important that you should keep it up during your lifetime. What time of day you run is not important as long as you run. In the beginning you should jog easily, then gradually increase the distance and tempo, and finally include sprinting to develop your wind."

Here we see both Bruce and his opponent in the classic ready for attack or defence poses of Kung-Fu. The attacker, to the left, holds his right hand at a 45° angle in the knife hand, or claw position. His left hand remains drawn back, prepared for palm heel blocking against any attacks made to his head or body. On the right, the defender holds both hands in the knife hand or claw position, with thumbs tucked in and all the fingers tensed for action. The left hand is held slightly lower, ready to block low line attacks to groin or stomach with knife hand or palm heel. Like his opponent, the defender holds his right hand forward at a 45° angle. This leaves him ready to block or deflect attacks on his head and shoulders while giving the immediate opportunity for counter-attacking.

This sequence illustrates an attack with the right hand thrust aimed at the head or body. The defence in this case is by using a right hand knife and block deflecting the attacker's forearm away and across the body. At the very instant of blocking, the defender's fingers are hooked onto his opponent's forward arm, thus pulling him forward and off balance, while a possible counter-attack shows a block and hooking movement. To deliver the right roundhouse kick, Lee bends his leg at the knee, lifts it up out to the side and holds it horizontal to the ground. Then, swivelling the hips, he swings the right foot around and kicks his opponent in the stomach with the ball of his foot. Also shows is another counter-attack — the side snap-kick. The knee is lifted and the foot is stamped straight out, delivering a blow to the opponent's armpit or ribcage.

Lee ran anything from two to six miles every day, often in the early morning. (Occasionally Linda, his wife, would be awoken in the dead of night by Lee setting out on a run, or vaulting over the furniture in the living room.) After he had finished an early morning workout, he would quietly return to bed. In Hong Kong, even when he was a movie super-star of extraordinary dimensions, he would always insist on embarking on a morning run and if he was spotted by fans he often had to sprint instead of jog.

Lee was also a great believer in using training equipment. As you can see, when the pictures in this book were taken Lee was not living in the most perfect accommodation for impromptu exercise. But even in his high-rise apartment he managed to construct an extremely serviceable gymnasium. In the living room he would practice his punching and kicking againt the punching pad his wife Linda held. Lee referred in Black Belt to his hands and feet as the tools of his trade which, by necessity, must be sharpened and improved each day in order to be efficient. This small kick-and-punch pad was perfect for cramped, indoor use.

Another piece of indoor equipment Lee utilised in his apartment was a construction of tubular steel shaped like a large chair turned on its back. With this Lee would strengthen and develop his lower abdominal muscles. After years of practice he was able to raise all of his body while lying in his shoulders, such was the enormous power of these lower muscles.

Lee managed to run through a complete fitness regimen on his small balcony - skip-

This sequence shows Bruce using a block and track technique with pressure against the joints. The attacker moves forward with a left hand thrust to the head and shoulders. Standing in the cat stance Lee moves forward himself, ducking underneath the blow and moving his own left hand under the attacker's arm towards his body. His right hand remains held back in the tiger's claw position, ready to strike. As the attacker tries to withdraw, Bruce immediately slides his left arm down his attacker's arm to grab his wrist. As soon as this has been done, he draws the attacker's left arm back with his own left arm and applies pressure from his palm heel to the shoulder, thus locking the arm straight out and rendering his opponent helpless. The final three pictures show the possible counter-attacks open to Lee once he has immobilised his opponent. Retaliation from a right hand blow to the face, the stomach or the solar plexus are all equally possible methods of counter-attack.

ping, push-ups, running-on-the-spot, high kicks, knee bends, sit-ups and so on. Even the balcony railing was used in his isometric exercises. (An isometric exercise is simply an exercise in which muscles are pitted against an immovable object to strengthen and develop them.) Lee would often stand for an hour pressing the backs of his hands against the railings as hard as he could. (To judge how much tension this adds to the muscles, try it yourself for a minute or two. Then step away and let your arms hang loosely by your sides. Automatically your arms will start to rise of their own accord. Now try it for an hour!)

Lee also constructed a portable gymnasium with make-shift equipment on his balcony. One of his favourite pieces of equipment was a combination of a chain and a spring which he used to help strengthen his arms and shoulders. Standing on the baseboard of this device, he would repeatedly draw the bar up to his chest. Another similar device was used to develop his hands and wrists. This involved grasping a bar from which various weights were hung and then drawing it up to a second bar.

When Lee became rich, he turned his homes into virtual gymnasiums. His home in Hong Kong was equipped with all the latest equipment he could lay his hands on. Fitness was an obsession with him, and he pursued it to the end regardless of expense.

Lee used isometrics to develop more than just arm muscles. One piece of equipment which he favoured and which was aimed at developing as many muscles as possible at once was the 'isometric bar.' This device, which was originated by Lee, consisted of a metal bar, heavily padded around the middle. The bar could be slotted at the desired height between two upright bars. Lee preferred to position the bar just below shoulder height. Then he would stoop under it, placing his shoulders and the back of his neck against the padding, and push upwards. This meant that calf, thigh, stomach and shoulder muscles could all be exercised at the same time. By placing his hands on the bar and exerting pressure with his arms at the same time, these also could be brought into play.

Lee also enjoyed working out on the fixed bicycle. For long periods of time he would pedal the equivalent of seven miles every other day on it.

In the gym, Lee worked several bags into his training. To achieve depth and penetration in his punches - and, sometimes, also his kicks - he used a bean bag. (In one of his homes in the early days he filled up most of his garage with an enormous bean bag). For Lee, the bean bag was ideal to practice his soft-hard techniques. Also, it gave a student the feeling of actually hitting a person.

He also relied heavily on the common 70 pound boxing bag. He used it chiefly to perfeet his timing, swinging the bag and attempting to gauge the correct split-second to launch the perfect kick. Another bag he incorporated in his training was the two-hundred-pound heavy bag, again to force himself to which teaches you to be alert and to recover correctly gauge height, distance and speed. One of the warnings he gave about 'fighting' a swinging bag was that because the bags did not respond aggressively as an opponent would, a student could become complacent and leave himself open while sparring. "Do not shove or poke at a bag," he warned. "Explode through it and remember that the power comes from the correct contact at the right spot and at the right moment with the body in perfect position, noy from the vigour with which the kicks or blows are delivered, as many people think."

Lee also liked to swing the heavy bag for another reason. "If I can stop it with one kick," he once laughed, "I know I can knock a four-hundred-pound man on his ass!"

Here the attacker moves forward with a left-handed blow to the defender's stomach, head or body. Lee blocks and tracks with the right hand and again he uses it to hook onto the attacker's forearm. With his opponent coming forward off balance, Lee is in an ideal situation to deliver his own attack either with a side snap-kick or an inside roundhouse kick to the head or the middle of his body.

This special sequence features Bruce Lee in just some of the free fighting techniques that have made him a worthy holder of the name 'Fist of Fury'. And judging by these pictures, 'Foot of Fury' as well! Lee illustrates the use of the side snap-kick against his opponent. The attacking foot is drawn up, bent at the knee, then thrust straight out using the side of the foot to the attack the side of the rib cage, under the armpit or into the stomach. Lee then shows how to perform a roundhouse kick, in this case using the right foot. The leg is lifted and bent at the knee until the knee is horizontal to the ground; then, by swivelling his hips, Lee can smash a devastating blow into his opponent's face. This technique, one of Bruce's hallmarks, is in fact very difficult to perform properly since it requires almost 180° spread of the legs. Not surprisingly, this kind of suppleness doesn't come without long and arduous practise. Lee performs a jumping side kick. Leaping into the air to reach the height of the intended kick, he draws up the left leg beneath the groin for added height. At the very peak of the jump this same foot is thrust straight out into the opponent's head. Obviously this skillful attack must be performed with maximum speed so as to strike the blow before the opponent can back off. Its advantage, of course, is the tremendous power that a leap and kick can give to the blow. This attack by itself can easily end any fight if it works. As Bruce's millions of movie fans will appreciate, he is indeed a master of this complex and powerful attack!

Another bag more commonly associated with boxing that Lee used was the speed bag. However, he preferred to use the old fashioned type of speed bag instead of the modern version. The new type served to tighten up timing and rhythms and to train a student to keep his hands held high. Yet Lee noted that no-one really fought like that. On other hand, the older, cord-supported the unity of his power. He also believed that it speed bag forced the student to punch straight and square. If he failed to do so, the bag would not return directly to him. Also, this type of bag allowed the student to hit upwards and taught him to use footwork. The speed bag was valuable, he noted in Black Belt Magazine, because "after the delivery of the punch, the bag will return instantaneously, which teaches you to be alert and to recover quickly." Also, he counselled, a student practising on the speed bag should punch out of rhythm in order to ensure a more human and realistic response.

As mentioned earlier, Lee was fond of using the round punching pad to practise his punches and kicks, especially his favourite hook kick to the face. The advantage of this pad was that it could be controlled by the person holding it. Height and distance could be altered in an instant. This meant that Lee had to be alert to movements in his target and make sure that he did not 'telegraph' his punches or kicks. The pad was, in his estimation, as close as possible to actual combat.

Another pad which Lee favoured was the jabbing pad. He used this to teach a student how to jab at an opponent's eyes. It was also beneficial in developing speed in jabbing; speed which, in Lee's case, was devastating.

Lee devised another unique aid to perfect speed - a paper target, hung from the ceiling by a piece of cord. By punching or kicking at this flimsy target, he could work on improving punching and side and hook kicking.

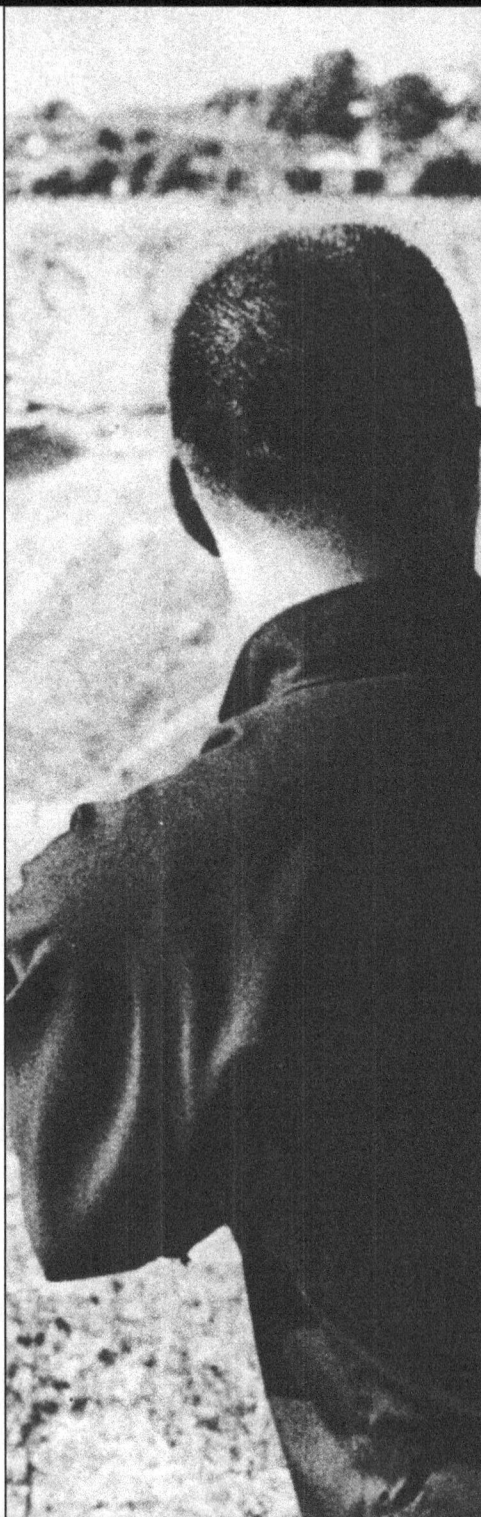

Here we can see Bruce Lee delivering a side snap-kick in absolutely perfect form. He uses the outside edge of his foot to smash a blow to his opponent's unprotected head. Notice how even as he goes into this devastating attack, his left hand is held in a fist position, making sure that his head and body are both securely covered in the event of any possible counter-attacks.

TRAINING WITH PARTNERS

As useful as these pads were, Lee knew that the perfect target was a human target. Lee regularly used an opponent equipped with either a body protector or an air bag in his workouts. As Lee attacked, this opponent would attempt to bade peddle, block or counter, benefiting both Lee - who would be confronted with a moving, irrational target - and himself, gaining expertise in defence tactics.

Unfortunately, Lee's 'all-out' punches and kicks often proved too much far even the most well-equipped opponent. Despite a body protector, Lee could land a blow which would leave an opponent gasping in pain. With seemingly no effort at all he could kick the most solid fighter literally across a room.

In order to really be able to fight 'all-out'. Lee constructed a unique piece of equipment, a wooden dummy. Wing Chun students had for many years practised on wooden dummies, but Lee's dummy was special. Taking the basic Wing Chun model, he refined it by add* ing his own pieces.

Lee's dummy stood six feet tall and had a diameter of some 12 inches. Below its 'neck', it had two removable 'hands', each measuring two feet in length. A third 'hand' was placed lower down. Lee used these 'hands' to practise blocking and punching as well as his famous 'sticking hands' exercise (a Wing Chun skill which, when mastered, allowed a fighter to follow an opponent's movements so closely that he could fight blindfolded). The dummy was mounted on a platform eight feet square and was supported by steel springs to give it movement. It had a single metal leg which ex-tended outwards and down. This leg was used for practising shin kicks and was instrumental in illustrating Lee's teachings that a fighter should always lock his opponent's leg with his own front leg in order to prevent him kicking.

Lee admitted that his dummy was not as good as the real thing. However, as it was virtually indestructible, he could thump it as hard as he wanted and it wouldn't fold up and collapse in a writhing heap on the floor.

But no matter how 'realistic' his dummy was, nor how fleet of foot his air-cushion-protected opponent might be, there was still no equal in Lee's training schedule for a proper sparring opponent. "Just because you get very good at this supplemental training," he warned in Black Belt, "it should not go to your head that you're an expert. Remember, actual sparring is the ultimate, and this training is only a means toward this."

"There is nothing better than freestyle sparring in the practice of any combative art. In sparring, you should wear suitable prote-tive equipment and go all out. Then you can truly learn the correct timing and distance for the delivery of the kicks, punches, etcetera. It is a good idea to spar with all types of individuals: short, tall, clumsy. Yes, at times a clumsy fellow will mess up a better man because his awkwardness serves as a sort of broken rhythm. "The best sparring partner, though, is a quick, strong man who does not know any-thing, a mad man who goes all out scratching, grabbing, punching and kicking."

For Lee, going 'all out' was supremely important when sparring. He had no time for 'styles' which only concentrated on one small element of fighting, elevating it to the exclusion of all other facets of combat. It was of the very essence of Lee's development as a martial artist that he was always determined to master the means whereby he could respond naturally to every move of his opponent no matter what was thrown at him. How,

questioned Lee, did all the different styles come about if, as many styles claimed, they could cope with all types of attack? Lee wasn't interested in segments; only in totality.

"Come in like a boxer would come in," he urged Dan Inosanto during sparring. "Come in swinging like a street fighter would swing."

Sparring was the height of teaming for Lee's Jeet Kune Do. Here on the combat floor there was no such thing as 'form' or 'style'. "Efficiency in sparring or fighting is not a matter of correct, classical, traditional form," he said. "Efficiency is anything that scores." To go ahead according to a fixed pattern learned by heart and create classical sets to replace freestyle sparring was, in his eyes, like "trying to wrap and tie a pound of water into the manageable shape of a paper sack."

"For something that is static, fixed, dead, there can be a way or a definite path, but not to anything that is moving and living. In sparring, there's no exact path or method but, instead, a perceptive, pliable, choiceless awareness. It lives from moment to moment." Similarly, the ancient controversy between 'hard' and 'soft', 'Internal' and 'External', was not important to Lee. He believed each was merely two halves of a whole. To concentrate on one at the risk of excluding the other was to miss out on the total form. One could not reject the firm and concentrate on the gentle, or vice-versa. All that could lead to was incompleteness.

As one author writing on Lee's art noted, Lee's training methods are not easy to present as a 'How to Keep Fit' textbook. Apart from the fact that his regimen was geared to the physical standards of his own extraordinary body, it was also in a constant state of flux, forever being adapted to Lee's needs of the moment. He could not tolerate a drill merely for its own sake.

"A martial artist who exclusively drills on a set pattern of combat is losing his freedom," said Lee. "He is actually becoming a slave to a choice pattern and feels that the pattern is the real thing. It leads to clogginess because the way of combat is never based on personal choice and fancies. Instead, it constantly changes from moment to moment, and the disappointed combatant will soon find out that his 'choice routine' lacks pliability. There must be a being instead of doing in training. One must be free." Free to change a drill if it didn't fit the requirements, free to adapt.

"Dan," he once told Inosanto, "if it doesn't work, throw it away. But you should drill on it first." If a drill was limited or re-strictive, he would find a way of adapting it to his own immediate needs: "Turn the stumbling block into a stepping stone." When he was injured in a car crash, he turned his whole regimen upside down - literally. Constructing a 'gravity' device, he hung himself upside down by the legs to stretch and exercise his damaged muscles. An extreme example of adaptability perhaps, but an example which shows the way in which his mind worked.

"The most important thing to me," said Lee, "is how, in the process of learning to use my body, can I come to understand myself."

STANCE

A correct stance is the foundation upon which Bruce Lee built his martial movements. He understood that if a fighter adopted a restrictive stance or 'telegraphed' his intentions to his opponent, then the fight would be over before it had started.

Lee taught that a fighter could not afford to pose himself in a set posture after each movement. Rather, he had to adopt the most natural position for that particular moment. This was the essence of Lee's thinking on stance. It was a golden rule that the "on guard' position had to be natural and relaxed, but at the same time leaving open the opportunity for the student to begin his range of offensive or defensive movements.

The 'on-guard' position was the core of Jeet Kune Do. Quite simply, it is the perfect defence posture. When a student has adopted it, he displays the least possible targets to an opponent. All movement should stem from the core position, taught Lee, and all movements should end with the fighter returning to the on-guard stance.

The secret of Lee's perfect stance was its balance. Lee felt that the student should lean slightly forward so that he is off the centre of gravity. This makes for a 'ready' position, similar to a stand-up start in a long distance race. According to Lee, the knees should be slightly bent to facilitate instant movement and quicker initial speed. The point of the chin must be protected by the collarbone of the leading arm. With the head tilted slightly down an opponent is denied a clear shot at the inviting chin target. In this position, only the top of the fighter's head is vulnerable.

Lee's insistence on remaining loose and relaxed becomes clear when a student begins an attack using his leading arm. If relaxed, this arm is able to snap out onto the target. On the other hand, if the guard is stiff and extended, then it will need to be contracted before the movement is undertaken. This in turn has the effect of 'telegraphing' the punch.

Lee's on-guard position also ensures maximum protection to the student. Each limb contributes to a comprehensive defensive cover: the leading hand and arm protect the face and body; the trailing shoulder and arm protect the face and ribs; the trailing hand protects the groin; the leading knee is turned to protect the groin. The head moves so as to present a moving and difficult target.

One other point that Lee made with regard to stance was that a student, on adopting the on-guard position, should be alert to the movements of his opponent which are away from the basic stance.

ESSENTIAL ELEMENTS

Bruce Lee formulated a number of attributes which he considered essential parts of Kung-Fu mastery. In his book Tao of Jeet Kune Do, Lee referred to these essential elements as 'Qualities.' If a student failed to develop these elements, in Lee's estimation he could be discounted as a complete fighter.

Perhaps the most basic of Lee's elements is co-ordination. As in all sports, co-ordination plays a large part in determing success and is especially true in Kung-Fu. Lee taught that a student lacking co-ordination would be unable to weld his power and ability into a unified action. Co-ordination permitted a fighter ease of movement and reduced muscle tension, he said. With co-ordination perfected, a fighter could 'out guess' his opponent, move deliberately into position with a minumum of effort and seize the initiative.

Lee wrote at length about the source of co-ordination. He believed it was derived by tuning the nervous system rather than through muscle training. Although a student's mus-

In this set of pictures, Bruce is demonstrating one of the more complex Kung-Fu kata (line forms). He has adopted the basic horse stance with the feet some two shoulders' widths apart and the knees slightly bent. The hands are held in the well-known sanchin position: both elbows cover the ribs, the hands are tightly clenched into fists and the forearms bend slightly outwards from the elbows. Lee's whole body is tensed in this position. The left foot is drawn slightly in and thus the body weight is mainly shifted on to it. The left hand drops into the tiger claw position to cover the solar plexus and the lower part of the head. The right hand is thrust forward into a two-finger spear position. Bruce Lee has adopted the snake creeping down position. His body weight has shifted almost entirely onto his back leg, which is bent at nearly 90° from his body. The left hand has dropped down slightly, and the forward hand's two-finger spear position has been slightly withdrawn and then, turned outwards to form a right-handed outside claw block. From this position the left foot is used to give a spring from which it is possible to leap forward. The next picture shows how the hands are held in the tiger claw defensive position after the left foot has crossed over to the right and the body has changed to its new position. The weight is mainly on the forward foot now, and the remaining 30% is on the back foot, which is bent. The final picture shows how the left hand can be moved forward from this position and thus a two-fingered spear thrust to the eyes or neck is possible.

cle development might still be superior to that of his opponent, he might nevertheless be far more unco-ordinated than the person he faced if his nervous system relayed signals to the wrong muscles, or if it signalled to slowly, wrote Lee. H taught that the nervous system was cmposed of billions of fibres which, when fused together, produced a pattern of co-ordination to which a fighter instinctively reacted. Lee considered that in order to train for co-ordination, a student had to practice moves and counter moves to encourage the fusing of these fibres and so provide a 'memory' pattern for instinctive movement.

The second element of Lee's perfect fighter was precision or accuracy. To encourage its development he advocated the use of a mirror during training so that a student could keep a check on the position and movement of hands, stance and technique.

Once precision had been developed, the student could then begin putting power into his skills. Lee recognized that maximum power was derived from the perfect welding of mechanical action to momentum - i.e. coordination. A powerful athlete, wrote Lee, is not necessarily a strong athlete, but one who can move swiftly. This meant that a smaller man who could punch or kick could generate more power than a heavier man who could only move slowly.

Speed, to Lee, was all-important and it was perhaps his most famous and devastating attribute. Although himself a small man, Lee boasted that he could beat any fighter in the world no matter what size. When colleagues qualified this statement after his death by adding the words, "pound-for-pound he probably could have", they were missing the point. Pounds had very little to do with Lee's strategy; his speed alone made them almostirrelevant.

Another important element linked with speed Lee called vision awareness - the ability to see something quickly. Lee wrote that skwmess of movement could be compensated by extra quickness with the eye.

He perfected accurate, immediate vision to such an extent that he could control the instinctive urge to blink when a punch or a kick was aimed at his face, and he urged his pupils to strive for the same ability. Vision aware-ness, be taught, came not from a basic animal instinct more pronounced in some than in others, but by learning. The student should train himself to cut down the number of 'choice-reactions' his eye was confronted with and learn to develop 'instinctive economy.' A student should also develop a reliance on his peripheral vision, he said. That is, he should try to take in a wide area with his vision rather than concentrate on small details of the wide picture.

Other types of speed (besides vision awareness) that Lee defined were speed of movement selection, speed in beginning a motion, speed in putting a chosen action into effect, and the ability of a student to alter or change position in midstream.

Lee taught that speed depended to an enormous degree on the economy of a fighter's movement, so, in order to become faster, each training movement had to be constantly repeated. For this Lee recommended shadow boxing.

Just how fast Lee himself became is illustrated by the following incidents, the first recounted by his friend, Adrian Marshall: "Bruce put this dime in my hand and then said, 'Let's see how fast you are - when I reach out for that dime, you close your fist and see if you can stop me from getting it.' Well, he moved once, and I closed by fist, and then he moved again, and once again I got my fist shut before he could grab the dime.

"The third time everything seemed to move a bit faster, but when I closed my fist, I still

Another left-handed attack on Lee. He chooses to block this one with a right-handed knife slash to the inside of the attacker's forearm. Moving to the offensive, he draws his right hand across the body and uses it to attack with a right-handed knife hand blow to the attacker's head or throat. Note the position of Lee's left hand. It is always held high across his body to make sure he is prepared to block any possible counter-attacks. In the final picture, the kn if eh and slashes down at a 45° angle into the opponent's collar or the side of his neck.

Exhibiting his usual perfection of form and balance, Bruce demonstrates a high roundhouse kick to the head. The knee is lifted approximately to chest height. Then the lower leg is brought out horizontal to the ground and in the final pictures, by swivelling his hips on the stand-ing leg, Bruce is able to deliver a stunning blow to his opponent's temple by slashing out in a wide arc with the ball of his foot.

In this superb series of action pictures Bruce performs one of the most complex of Kung-Fu's formal exercises, the kata. The sequence begins with his starting position for this exercise. The feet are about one shoulder width apart, the weight is evenly distributed, the hands are by the sides. The right hand is bent inwards at the wrist and the arm is straightened and thrust forward to perform a wrist block with the right wrist. The left hand is moved to the tiger claw position. Bruce Lee then executes a left-handed block against an imaginary attacker's straight thrust by using the outside edge of his forearm. In the following picture, he adopts the horse stance, hands in tiger claw position using the right one to guard his groin and the left as a cover for possible attacks on the torso or the face. He then moves from the tiger claw position into the double wrist block position and the next picture shows this wrist block lifting an imaginary attacker's arms high up and outwards. After repulsing his mythical opponent, Lee now moves into an attack stance. The next series of pictures feature a demonstration of tension wrist techniques. This sequence of slowly formed blocks and knife hand techniques should not be performed at speed but at extreme tension. It is designed especially to strengthen the muscles of both arms and wrists, and will contribute at the same time to developing the balance and poise. Note that the basic stance here is the cat position, with 70% of the weight resting on the back foot. The bext pictures illustrate a further series of strengthening movements which are performed with extreme tension in the muscles of the arms and legs. The left hand is pulled back to cover the face with the palm and

the right hand moves downwards to form a wrist block with the outside edge of the wrist. This will parry a possible low line attack. From this position the right arm is drawn back to cover the body and the left drops to protect the groin. The final picture of this sequence is Bruce Lee's finishing stance. Both hands are in the tiger claw position, the right is high to cover the head while the left drops down to take care of the groin and lower torso. The right knee is drawn up into what is commonly known as the crane stance, or sometimes as the golden rooster standing on one leg position. From this position a side snap kick can easily be performed. Also from this final position, the whole exercise can be simply recommenced by moving back to the stance shown in the first picture.

had that dime tightly clutched. Or at least I thought I hadl When I opened my fist, not only had the dime gone - there was a penny lying in my hand instead."

Another favourite party trick of Lee's was to ask a friend to hold his or her hand up by their face, ready to stop Lee's movements. What he had to do was attempt to close their eyelids with his fingers without being intercepted. Not only was he never caught, he closed the eyelids without his friend feeling anything!

As with speed, Lee, in his Tao of Jeet Kune Do, broke timing down into a series of more detailed definitions. Reaction time, he wrote, was the time taken between a movement - 'stimulus' - and a student's response to that movement. Movement time was the time taken to execute a motion. Lee wrote that a fighter could cut down an opponent's movement time by disturbing his rhythm, immobilizing him, forcing him to provide an initial reaction which could be acted upon, and by avoiding or deflecting his movement. Timing, stressed Lee, was the secret of powerful hitting.

Lee invented a blow which relied almost solely on timing. The punch, which he labelled a 'stop-hit' was an attack made against an opponent who was himself in the process of attacking. Essentially, it aimed to break up this attack before it was properly formulated. Lee found it especially useful against an opponent who attacked wildly without too much regard to covering himself.

Endurance was another of Lee's pre-requisites. He taught that it could be attained best by a student's 'performance of the event', together with additional exercises included on the supplementary training schedule. A student must work himself hard, rest adequately, and then work himself even harder, counselled Lee.

As mentioned previously, balance was another consideration uppermost in Lee's mind when he was planning strategy. "Without balance at all times," he wrote, "he (the fighter) can never be effective." Correct balance was derived from a correct stance, he taught. It could be achieved by keeping the feet directly beneath the body and a medium distance apart. In Western boxing, the fighter's weight is balanced over both legs, but to Lee the best position was obtained by putting the weight slightly over the lead leg, with its slightly bent knee. The heel of the lead foot should be just touching the ground. Weight should be kept on the balls of the feet and the centre of gravity kept low. Lee taught that this centre of gravity had to be kept under control, even though the secret of his art was in throwing this centre around - tilting it forward, back or to the side and then bringing it under the control of the base support again by a short step, a glide or some other movement.

Lee's command of balance can best be seen in his film Way of the Dragon during his epic fight against Chuck Norris in the Coliseum. The first part of this fight - the part which has Norris winning against his small opponent - is notable for Lee's search for balance. Unable to develop a rhythm against Norris, he is caught many times by the American Karate champion. Then Lee discovers his centre of gravity, begins moving on his own terms rather than as a defensive response to Norris' attacks, and goes on to win the day.

Other points that Lee emphasized were relaxation, of prime importance in eliminating wasted energy, and the attitude of a fighter. Lee called the ability to distinguish between muscle contraction and relaxation 'kinesthetic perception*. By being able to reproduce the feeling of relaxation at will - especially in 'tension-creating' situations - the fighter would be able to cut energy loss to a minimum, Lee said. If muscles were overly tense, then speed and skill were impossibly handicapped.

As to attitude, Lee recognized that a fighter needed what he termed a 'winning attitude.' This, he said, was comprised of self-confidence plus a lack of excess tension. Emotional control was, for Lee, essential.

ATTACK

Of all the elements of combat that Lee covered in his instruction, he dwelt longest on the tactics of attack. In his Tao ofJeet Kune Do, Lee sets down - in what is probably his most complete chapter - a detailed analysis of attack. Among other aspects he lists "The Psychophysical Process of Attack', primary and secondary attack, preparation, simple and compound attack, counter-attack and tactics ... all in all, 29 full pages.

But for all of this, Lee's instruction was merely elaboration of two very basic elements. This fact was admirably captured in a quote the compilers of the Tao included as a prelude to die chapter on attack: "There is nothing much in this art. Take things as they are. Punch when you have to punch; kick when you have to kick." To Lee, a master of attack was basically a master of the kick and the punch.

Together with these, Lee's most devastating and spectacular attribute was speed. Indeed, one of the several nicknames given him by awed opponents, incredulous spectators and envious pupils was 'the man with three legs', a direct reference to his staggering control over his feet.

Lee's phenomenal kicks were born in the gymnasium from a strenuous set of leg exercises. As a student, as soon as he had developed his muscles sufficiently, he graduated to such formidable exercises as kicking trees. "When you can kick so you aren't jarred but the tree is jarred," he said, "then you will begin to understand a kick." Of course the power generated by such exercises was extraordinary. When practising his favourite backward hook-kicks, Lee would often direct a colleague to hold onto the bottom of the heavy bag to give him more resistance. When Lee kicked, the man would invariably be hurled across the room by the sheer force produced.

As with punching, Lee believed that a fighter had to 'become one' with his kick. "The secret of kicking as Bruce taught it," recalled Danny Inosanto on one occasion, "was controlled anger. I remember once he asked me to try kicking. He held this shield and for five minutes I kicked at that shield, desperately trying to improve my kick. I really thought I was giving my all - but Bruce wasn't satisfied. Finally he came over and slapped me on the face, at the same time calling out, 'Now, kick! He held up the shield - I was simply blazing with anger and went ROW! It was fantastic!"

Lee's range and variety of kicks was dazzling. La his Tao he lists no less than forty-eight 'Leg Techniques', broken down into Side Kicks, Leading Straight Kick, Reverse Straight Kick. Hook Kick, Spin Back Kick, Hooking Heel Kick and Knee Thrust. His list of kick targets on an opponent's body - as Chester Maydole mentioned in the introduction to this book - is equally as comprehensive.

In the Tao, Lee takes pains to point out that the development and employment of power in a kick is all-important. He warns against students falling into the habit of "flicking9 at an opponent with the foot. He instructed that a happy medium had to be found by the student which enabled him to use his power at the fastest possible speed.

Lee further broke down his kicks into long and short range movements. Long range he

These six pictures are a selection from another of Bruce's exercises, the ten-sho kata. This entire kata is performed in the sanchin stance. Both elbows cover the ribs, the hands are tightly clenched into fists and the forearms bend out slightly from the elbows. This kata is performed very slowly with maximum tension, particularly on the stomach muscles, since the central feature of the whole exercise is breathing. The first pictures show a wrist block being performed. In the next pictures, Bruce demonstrates his method of breaking the theoretical hold that an opponent has on his collar or jacket. This is done by crossing the arms and then slashing outwards with both hands to break the hold, then turning to offense and striking out at the opponent's neck with a knife hand. The sanchin stance, in which this kata is performed is also known as the 'pigeon-toe' stance. As well as the tension in the arms, the legs create a great tension in the lower body. One foot is held slightly in front of the other, both feet are at 45° to the body with heels out-

wards and toes pointing in. The knees are slightly bent and pull in towards each other to promote the greatest tension possible. This kata is mainly intended to be a breathing exercise. One breath is taken before every move: it is drawn in sharply through the nose, then held down, pushed onto the diaphragm, held for some seven seconds and then exhaled through the mouth under tension while the move is actually in progress. Each movement of this kata takes some five seconds.

used primarily to reach a target at a distance from him, of course, but he also used them as a means of filling up a gap between opponents so as to cover a follow-up kick or punch.

Kung-Fu - and especially Lee's own brand, Jeet Kune Do - is naturally, a potentially lethal means of self-defence. Nowhere is this fact more evident than in Lee's instruction on kicking. In the Tao, Lee urges his students to study such things as 'kicking while a man is down', a concept that is anathema to 'sport', both Western and Eastern. Lee goes even further than this, listing in the Tao various means of immobilizing an opponent who is on the ground. Some of his methods include: kicking an opponent in the temple; performing a knee drop to the head, solar plexus and groin; and stomping the heel onto an opponent's face or rib cage. In cold print these tactics appear sickeningly callous. However they

As well as the formal exercises - kata - which Bruce used to keep at top form for his Kung-Fu fighting, he also appreciated the great importance of other forms of more general physical exercise. This picture, taken on the balcony of Bruee's Hong Kong flat, shows him working out to keep at peak fitness all the time. Bruce is using a simple lifting apparatus, loaded with 50 kilo weights.

serve to illustrate the basic precept of Jeet Kune Do: win at all cost.

For punching, Lee taught along roughly the same basic lines as he used for kicking. Perhaps his most famous quote on the martial arts urged that a fighter had to live each punch, becoming the movement as it was made. "At the moment you punch you must really be in with that punch," he told numerous people.

To reach a stage of 'oneness' with a punch required many hours in the gymnasium. As with kicking, the development of power in a punch was of prime importance to Lee. The extent to which he developed power in his own punches can best be judged by one of his better known 'party tricks' - the one-inch punch. This demonstration, which Lee used regularly in his many promotional exhibitions, required an opponent to stand directly in front of Lee. Lee would then reach out his arm until his fist was only a bare inch away from his opponent's chest. Then he would punch across that inch. Before the demonstration he would wager that he could throw his opponent across the room with a one-inch punch, no matter how tall or heavy the opponent might be. He never failed to accomplish his boast.

Although he listed several methods of striking in the Tao (including a variety of hooks), Lee held that the punch fundamental to Jeet Kune Do was the leading straight punch. Although primarily an offensive weapon, it was also useful as a defensive weapon, he taught. Its power came from the whole body and not, as with traditional Kung-Fu, from the hip.

Lee cautioned against the student adopting a formal stand-off position before taking a punch or any other similar attacking move. Rather, the punch should be developed so that it can be taken from wherever the a hand happens to be at a particular time. This led to speed and helped prevent the student 'telegraphing' his intentions to his opponent, Lee wrote that, like Western boxers, the Jeet Kune Do master punched through his target rather than at it. To gain power, the student must have a Working knowledge of body leverage so that the body and legs could transmit their energy. In fact, Lee wrote, arm action itself was not enough to provide sufficient power; the body must have a working knowledge that the hip and shoulder precede the arm to the centre line of the body." In the accompanying photographs, this position can be clearly seen.

As mentioned previously, there were many more facets to Lee's teaching on attack. He devoted more space in his Tao to the discussion of tactics - 'the brain-work of fighting.' The tactics of fighting consisted of preliminary analysis, preparation and execution, and the aim of tactics was to spot and take advantage of an opponent's weaknesses. However, to fully represent Lee's ideas on tactics and other aspects of attack would take much more space than is available here. The essential elements of Lee's attack were simply punching and kicking, and if the student of the martial arts masters these then Jeet Kune Do is within his grasp.

This picture shows Bruce Lee in a contemplative mood enjoying one of the many volumes that make up his famous martial arts library. While all of Bruce's legions of fans have come to know the Little Dragon for his unrivalled skills in Kung-Fu, Lee himself had something of a reputation amongst fellow enthusiasts for his near-encyclopedic knowledge of the martial arts.

THE WORLD FAMOUS
MARKETPLACE

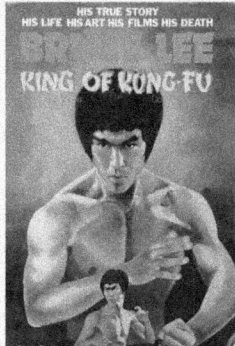

◀ BRUCE LEE
KING OF KUNG FU

Written by Felix Dennis & Don Atyeo, Bruce Lee King of Kung Fu is the original and still one of the greatest books on Bruce Lee ever written. Packed with photos and essential information from the immediate year after Lee's tragic death, Bruce Lee King of Kung Fu provides the best of rock-solid backgrounds to the story of the man we all know and love.
170 PAGES

KUNG-FU MONTHLY ▶
THE POSTER MAGAZINES

Volume One - No. 1 to 25, trade dummy plus an in-depth article on The History of Kung-Fu Monthly 1973 to 1979.
Volume Two - No. 26 to 55 plus interviews with former KFM staff.
Volume Three - No. 56 to 79, double-poster special edition issue plus an in-depth article on The History of Kung-Fu Monthly 1980 to 1984.

540-670 PAGES

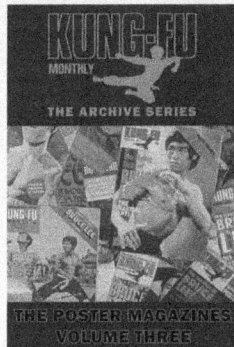

THE BOOK OF ▶
KUNG FU

The Book of Kung Fu was to be Kung-Fu Monthly's special annual issue, but was only published in 1974. Over one-hundred pages, many of them in colour, with a durable soft cover and scores of photographs, illustrations and articles. Don't miss this book! Bruce Lee, Angela Mao, David Carradine, Kung Fu Quiz, Comic Book and more - an incredible publication!
144 PAGES

THE SECRET ART OF ▶
BRUCE LEE

In 1976, the world took its first look at the now legendary Chester Maydole photographs. Arranged where possible, in 'fast-frame' action sequences, The Secret Art of Bruce Lee shows the founder of Jeet Kune Do, assisted by his friend and student Dan Inosanto, demonstrating the early development state of his art Jeet Kune Do during early days in Los Angeles.
110 PAGES

THE WISDOM OF BRUCE LEE
The History Of His Life And Jeet Kune Do

Special Edition by F. Dennis and R. Hutc...

THE KUNG-FU MONTHLY ARCHIVE

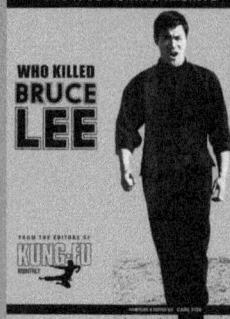

THE WISDOM OF BRUCE LEE

FELIX DENNIS
ROGER HUTCHINSON

THE 'LOST' KFM BOOK

NEVER BEFORE RELEASED IN THE UK

THE WISDOM OF BRUCE LEE

The Wisdom of Bruce Lee was to be one of the first books in the world to look at Bruce Lee's philosophy on life and martial arts. Mysteriously never released in the UK, The Wisdom of Bruce Lee is finally available to UK Bruce Lee fans after a wait of over forty years.

The full-length version includes a new introduction and interview with author Roger Hutchinson by Jun Fan Journal writer Andrew Staton, while the shorter abridged version is formatted in the style of the original Kung-Fu Monthly books.
70 PAGES / 170 PAGES

THE KUNG FU MONTHLY ARCHIVE

THE UNBEATABLE BRUCE LEE

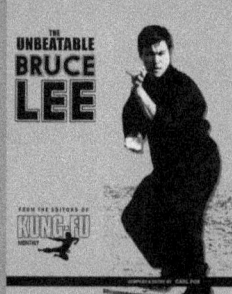

THE UNBEATABLE BRUCE LEE

The Unbeatable Bruce Lee presents readers with a fighter's view of Bruce Lee the man and Bruce Lee the martial arts master. Beneath the sheer weight of known facts and figures that surround the tragically short life of Hong Kong's number one son, lies a strata of truth that only now is beginning to be picked.
112 PAGES

THE KUNG FU MONTHLY ARCHIVE

BRUCE LEE IN ACTION

BRUCE LEE IN ACTION

With Bruce Lee in Action, the Editors of Kung-Fu Monthly had compiled another fine addition to their library of Bruce Lee publications. Lavishly illustrated throughout with many previously unseen photographs at the time, this informative book investigates clearly and concisely, the birth and subsequent development of Lee's fighting style Jeet Kune Do, both on and off the screen.
106 PAGES

THE POWER OF BRUCE LEE

THE KUNG FU MONTHLY ARCHIVE

THE POWER OF BRUCE LEE

Bruce Lee was possibly the greatest exponent of the martial arts ever produced. The fact that he was a movie star often clouds his enormous contribution to the field. The Power of Bruce Lee explores many of his revolutionary methods of attack and defence, especially those relating to Jeet Kune Do, Lee's name for his own fighting system
110 PAGES

WHO KILLED BRUCE LEE?

THE KUNG FU MONTHLY ARCHIVE

WHO KILLED BRUCE LEE

Who Killed Bruce Lee? is a study of the pressures and the forces that, on the one hand were to elevate him to the highest plains of stardom and on the other, were to so tragically strike him down before his final fulfilment.

Who Killed Bruce Lee? was one of the first books to delve deep into the newspaper stories of Lee's early death.
108 PAGES

THE GAME OF DEATH

This book combines two Kung-Fu Monthly special edition magazines released prior to Golden Harvest's 1978 film. Researched exclusively in Hong Kong, Kung-Fu Monthly reports on Lee's plot for Game of Death, the cast he intended to appear in the film, the scenes already filmed and Lee's hopes and expectations for the success of the project.Incredibly accurate for the time, this publication represents an important part of Bruce Lee fandom in the UK.
XXX PAGES

FIND OUT MORE INFORMATION AT

THE MAGAZINES

WWW.KUNGFUMONTHLY.UK

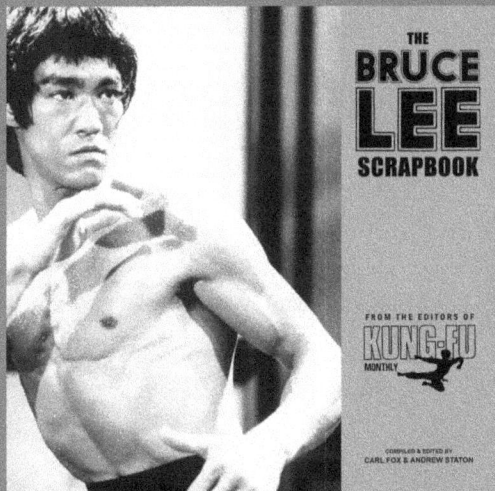

FROM THE EDITORS OF

COMPILED & EDITED BY
CARL FOX & ANDREW STATON

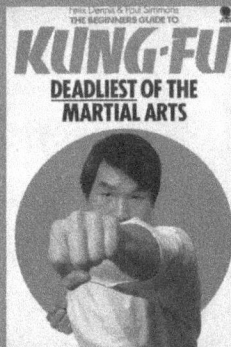

◄ THE BEGINNER'S GUIDE TO KUNG FU

Originally released in 1974, The Beginner's Guide to Kung Fu was the first martial arts book aimed primarily at the Kung Fu Craze generation. The graphic, easy to understand illustrations by Paul Simmons and the carefully conceived step by step instructions made this the perfect book for beginners who wished to take up Kung Fu.
XXX PAGES

THE BRUCE LEE SCRAPBOOK

In 1974, Kung-Fu Monthly issued a Bruce Lee scrapbook in the form of a large A3 magazine, followed by a smaller A4 sized book in 1979.
As part of the KFM Archive Series, both scrapbooks have been combined in a new chronological layout with brand new captions, location information and dates by Carl Fox and Jun Fan Journal writer Andrew Staton.
150 PAGES

THE KFM BRUCE LEE SOCIETY ►

Long before the internet communities we know today, The Bruce Lee Society was the source of information in the United Kingdom for all things Bruce Lee.Now the history of the Bruce Lee Society is finally told in The Bruce Lee Society: A Retrospective Look at Bruce Lee Mania and the Kung Fu Craze of the 1970s. For the first time ever, all thirty issues of The Bruce Lee Society newsletters have been painstakingly re-edited and re-printed in this book, along with updated notes and retrospective stories by the people most responsible for keeping Bruce Lee's memory alive - the fans.
544 PAGES

FOLD-OUT BRUCE LEE POSTER INSIDE
PAGES OF FANTASTIC ACTION PIX
KUNG-FU MONTHLY
BRUCE LEE
AND THE SAVAGING OF THE MAD CLAW
EXCLUSIVE What was BRUCE LEE Really Like?
FOLD OUT POSTER!
KFM SALUTES BRUCE LEE'S 4TH ANNIVERSARY!
UNBEATABLE JEET KUNE DO
WHERE IS THE MAGIC

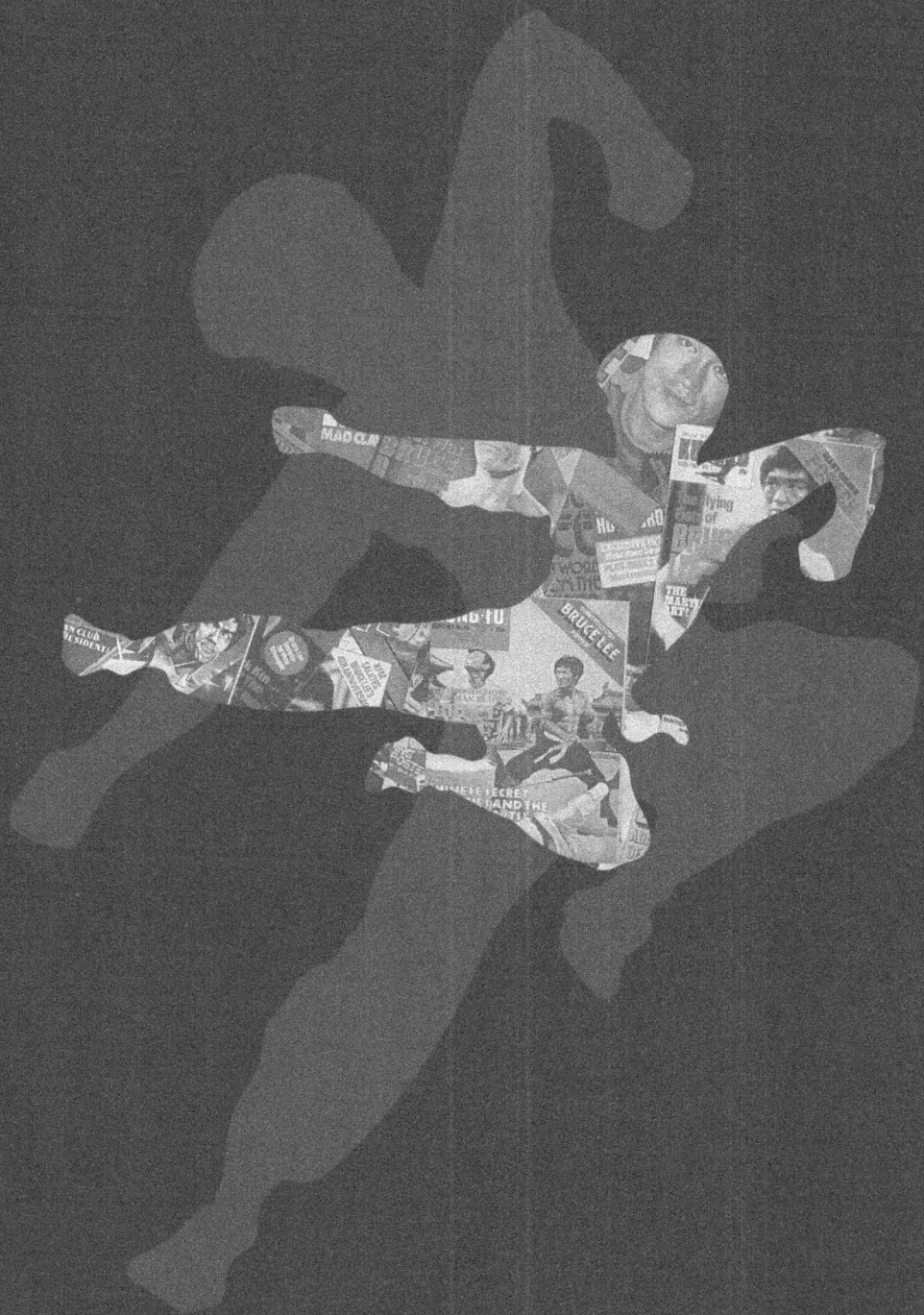